THE P.R.I.M.E.R. GOAL SETTING METHOD

THE ONLY GOAL ACHIEVEMENT GUIDE YOU'LL EVER NEED!

DAMON ZAHARIADES

ARTOFPRODUCTIVITY.COM

CONTENTS

OTHER BOOKS BY DAMON ZAHARIADES

The Art of Letting GO

Finally let go of your anger, regrets, and negative thoughts and enjoy the emotional freedom you deserve!

The Mental Toughness Handbook

The definitive, step-by-step guide to developing mental toughness! Exercises included!

To-Do List Formula

Finally! Discover how to create to-do lists that work!

The Art Of Saying NO

Are you fed up with people taking you for granted? Learn how to set boundaries, stand your ground, and inspire others' respect in the process!

The Procrastination Cure

Discover how to take quick action, make fast decisions, and finally overcome your inner procrastinator!

Fast Focus

Here's a proven system that'll help you to ignore distractions, develop laser-sharp focus, and skyrocket your productivity!

The 30-Day Productivity Plan

Need a daily action plan to boost your productivity? This 30-day guide is the solution to your time management woes!

The 30-Day Productivity Plan - VOLUME II

30 MORE bad habits that are sabotaging your time management - and how to overcome them one day at a time!

How to Make Better Decisions

Learn how to finally overcome indecision and make smart, effective choices without fear or regret!

The Time Chunking Method

It's one of the most popular time management strategies used today. Triple your productivity with this easy 10-step system.

80/20 Your Life!

Achieve more, create more, and enjoy more success. How to get more done with less effort and change your life in the process!

Small Habits Revolution

Change your habits to transform your life. Use this simple, effective strategy for adopting any new habit you desire!

Morning Makeover

Imagine waking up excited, energized, and full of self-confidence. Here's how to create morning routines that lead to explosive success!

The Joy Of Imperfection

Finally beat perfectionism, silence your inner critic, and overcome your fear of failure!

Digital Detox

Disconnect to reconnect. Discover how to unplug and enjoy a more mindful, meaningful, and rewarding life!

For a complete list, please visit

http://artofproductivity.com/my-books/

YOUR FREE GIFT

~

As my way of saying thank you for purchasing *The P.R.I.M.E.R. Goal Setting Method*, I'd like to offer you my 40-page action guide titled *Catapult Your Productivity! The Top 10 Habits You Must Develop To Get More Things Done.*

It's in PDF format, so you can print it out easily and read it at your leisure. This guide will show you how to develop core habits that'll help you to get more done in less time.

You can grab your copy by clicking on the following link and joining my mailing list:

http://artofproductivity.com/free-gift/

You'll also receive periodic tips for overcoming procrastination, developing effective morning routines, sharpening your focus, and more!

On that note, let's get started. I have a feeling you're going to love what you find in *The P.R.I.M.E.R. Goal Setting Method*.

PREFACE

My love affair with goal setting started as a child. Back then, my goals were little more than wishes. I desired something specific to happen (for example, I wanted my parents to take me to the arcade) or I wanted to acquire something (a new video game). Unfortunately, I was stymied regarding the steps I needed to take to achieve these "goals."

Many adults approach goal setting in a similar manner. They identify something they want - for example, to retire at 60 years of age - but fail to create a practical plan to make it happen. *The P.R.I.M.E.R. Goal Setting Method* addresses the second part of this process.

My Long, Frustrating Road To Success

Goal achievement has been an exasperating experience for me. It has been rapturous in times of success and vexing in times of failure. Over three decades, I've struggled to learn what works and what doesn't, and failed more times than I bear to remember.

My biggest stumbling block? I was ignorant about the factors that determine success and failure. I was clueless regarding why I managed to achieve *some* goals and failed to achieve others.

That's no longer the case. Over the years, I've run just about every test you can imagine to figure out the "secret" to goal achievement. The result is a surprisingly simple goal-setting system that all but ensures success.

You'll learn this system, from start to finish, in the following pages.

What Do You Want To Achieve?

Maybe you'd like to improve your interpersonal skills. Perhaps you'd like to get into shape. Maybe you'd like to get a better job, declutter your home, save more money, or start a side business.

All of us have aspirations that stem from our circumstances and desires. We want to better our lives in measurable ways. Setting goals is the first step toward doing so.

The problem is, *setting* goals is the easy part. The *hard* part is consistently achieving them. Whether our goals are related to our careers, relationships, health, wealth, or just plain happiness, many folks almost *expect* to fail. They've conditioned themselves with such expectations.

We can do better. *Much* better.

Failure Is Not An Option

Technically, failure is *always* an option. But it doesn't have to be if you use the P.R.I.M.E.R. goal setting method. You can literally achieve any goal you set.

Fair warning: work is involved. Although my P.R.I.M.E.R. method is simple, it's not magic. You'll need to set the right type of goals, create a practical action plan, and then focus on execution. Don't worry about these things right now. We're going to cover each of them in detail.

The most important thing to remember is that *you* control outcomes. *You* decide whether or not you achieve your goals. You're in the driver's seat. I'll show you which gears to engage, when to engage them, and how to use them to their greatest cumulative effect. But ultimately, *you're* in charge.

Your Mission, If You Choose To Accept It...

Are you ready to create and achieve goals that'll lead to a more rewarding life? Are you ready to take the reins of your destiny and exert your influence, transforming your lifestyle in the process?

I'll give you the blueprint in *The P.R.I.M.E.R. Goal-Setting Method*. Your job is to take action and monitor the results.

We're in this together.

Let's roll up our sleeves and "prime" the pump.

LAYING THE FOUNDATION FOR OUR GOAL-SETTING STRATEGY

～

Before we get into the nuts and bolts of my goal-setting system, we first need to talk about some foundational concepts. These concepts are probably intuitive to you. But they're also easy to overlook. And if you overlook them, you could very well sabotage your success.

Below, we'll cover five core tactics that align with how the brain works. By using them, we'll essentially "trick" our minds into helping us attain our goals. Each of these tactics is simple, but highly effective.

Assign A Reason Why For Each Goal

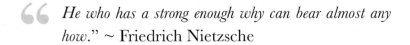

> *He who has a strong enough why can bear almost any how.*" ~ Friedrich Nietzsche

Having a reason gives us purpose. It clarifies why we want to accomplish something. When we're tempted to give up, it encourages us to press onward.

For example, suppose your goal is to lose 25 pounds. Without a compelling reason, there's little to spur you to exercise or eat healthily when you lack motivation. But let's say you want to lose 25 pounds in order to fit into a wedding dress on your wedding day. That's a compelling reason that'll help you to persevere.

It's important that your reason is specific. For example, it's not enough to say you'd like to lose 25 pounds to be healthier. That's too vague. It's much easier to stick to goals that are inspired by distinct reasons.

Your reasons don't have to focus on positive outcomes. Negative outcomes can be just as effective. For example, you might want to quit smoking to avoid developing lung cancer. You may want to save a certain sum of money to avoid bankruptcy in the event of a costly medical emergency.

Assign a specific reason to each goal. Leverage the potential for both positive outcomes and negative outcomes to stay focused and inspired.

Write Down Your Goals

 Goals that are not written down are just wishes." ~ Fitzhugh Dodson

I neglected to use this tactic for years. And it definitely hurt my success. Storing goals in my head allowed me to delude myself into thinking I was making forward progress on them. But in fact, that assumption was a mirage. Worse, my brain was given the freedom to distort my goals according to how I was feeling in the moment.

For example, my intent to save money was easily abandoned whenever I felt like spending money on a new gadget. My intent to do 100 pushups a day was easily abandoned whenever I felt lazy.

Writing down goals encourages us to take consistent action. It expresses our purpose and intention. And importantly, it eliminates the latitude our brains would otherwise use to dissuade us from our desired outcomes whenever the going gets tough.

Write down every goal you set for yourself. Do it on paper or do it online. It's your choice. Many goal-setting apps, such as Strides and HabitHub (both offer free versions), are terrific for this purpose. You can even use task management apps like Todoist and Trello.

Identify Limiting Beliefs

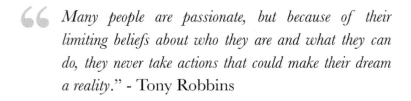 *Many people are passionate, but because of their limiting beliefs about who they are and what they can do, they never take actions that could make their dream a reality."* - Tony Robbins

Limiting beliefs represent how we perceive ourselves and our place in the world around us. They're comprised of negative self-talk, excuses, rationalizations, fear, and justifications for past failures. The outcomes we experience, both positive and negative, largely stem from these beliefs.

For example, suppose you fear that everyone lies. Can you imagine how this limiting belief might prevent you from finding a loving life partner? Or suppose you feel you're not smart enough to get a promotion at your job. Can you see how this belief might hamper your ability to advance your career?

Limiting beliefs act like toxins to goals. They poison your mindset, making you less likely to succeed. So it's crucial that you identify and overcome them prior to setting goals.

The simplest way to do this is to ask yourself the following three questions...

- What self-defeating assumptions have I made regarding my abilities?

- When do I typically experience fear, nervousness, agitation, or doubt?
- What self-critical narratives do I entertain as truth without evidence?

Write down your answers. Then, question the veracity of each one. Here are a few examples…

Limiting belief: No one is interested in what I have to say.
Question: Has anyone ever listened to you? If so, they were interested in what you had to say.

Limiting belief: I can't lose weight.
Question: Have you ever managed to lose weight in the past? If so, you can definitely do it again.

Limiting belief: I can't do it because I'm not tech savvy.
Question: Can you learn a new skill? If so, the issue isn't whether you *can or can't* do it. It's whether you *will or won't* do it.

Your beliefs influence your mindset, which in turn influences your actions. Identify and overcome your limiting beliefs, and I guarantee you'll see better results.

Set A Deadline For Each Goal

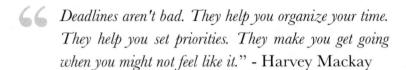 *Deadlines aren't bad. They help you organize your time. They help you set priorities. They make you get going when you might not feel like it."* - Harvey Mackay

Deadlines make our goals feel more substantive. They also create a sense of urgency. We're more inclined to take action when deadlines loom in the distance. So, it pays to assign a deadline to every goal.

Deadlines are sometimes baked into the goals themselves. For example, suppose you want to retire by the time you turn 60. Or let's say you aspire to lose 25 pounds by your wedding day. In both cases, the deadlines are already set.

Other times, you'll need to set them from scratch, if only to prevent a goal from remaining open-ended. For example, suppose you'd like to visit the Bahamas. Rather than hoping to do so "someday," commit to doing so by next summer. Put a deadline on it. You'll be more inclined to make it happen.

Deadlines keep us accountable to ourselves. They keep us moving forward and give us the discipline to ignore lower-priority desires. They also allow us to set up milestones to ensure we stay on the right track.

Create A Process That Supports Each Goal

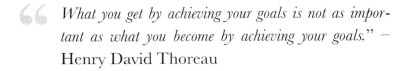 *What you get by achieving your goals is not as important as what you become by achieving your goals." –* Henry David Thoreau

It's not enough to focus on outcomes and deadlines. You must also focus on *process*.

Process is the path you travel toward your destination. For example, if your goal is to lose 25 pounds by your wedding day, your process will likely include your diet and exercise regimen.

Some experts advocate ignoring goals altogether, instead focusing solely on processes (or systems). In my opinion, it's beneficial to focus on goals *and* processes. First, decide where you'd like to end up. Then, once you've identified your destination, create habits that guarantee your success.

For example, suppose you'd like to retire by 60. After researching historical investment returns, inflation, assumed expenditures, and your life expectancy, you decide that you'll need $1.5 million in savings to achieve this goal.

We now have our destination. Having identified this goal, we can now work backwards and formulate a process. Let's suppose that based on your age, annual income, and current savings, you determine that you'll need to save $2,500 a month to accumulate $1.5 million by age 60. You now have a plan.

The next step is to develop the savings *habit*.

Again, I strongly encourage you to focus on both goals *and* processes. Focusing on one to the exclusion of the other risks failure. We'll talk in greater detail later about how these two aspects work together.

The next section will give you a bird's-eye view of what you'll find in *The P.R.I.M.E.R. Goal Setting Method*.

A BRIEF TOUR OF THE P.R.I.M.E.R. GOAL SETTING METHOD

~

There's a science to effective goal setting. There's also an art to it. This book will teach you both aspects, and do so in a way that allows you to start seeing results almost immediately.

If you've glanced through the table of contents, you'll have noticed that we have a lot of material to cover. We're going to go through it quickly. My goal is to take you through the material in just a couple of hours. In my opinion, there's no better way to learn how to do something than to *actually do it*. So we're going to spend minimal time on the science of goal setting. Instead, we'll focus on actionable steps you can take *today*.

This book is organized into four parts. Following is what you'll learn in each of them.

Part I

Tactical errors are the most common cause of failure when it comes to goal achievement. The problem is, such errors are usually subtle and difficult to recognize. They can sabotage you without your realizing they're doing so.

Part I will spotlight the most pivotal mistakes people make when setting goals. You'll learn how to avoid them, and immediately improve your success rate in the process.

Part II

There are many goal-setting strategies in use today. Some are quite good while others introduce significant problems.

Part II will describe the 10 most popular strategies, highlighting their respective strengths and weaknesses. This is an important section because it clarifies and underscores the reasons my P.R.I.M.E.R. goal setting method is effective.

Part III

Once you have a firm grasp on today's most popular goal-setting systems, I'll introduce you to my P.R.I.M.E.R. method.

Part III will take you, step by step, through the entire process. We'll take a close look at why each step is critical to your success, and come up with an action plan you can put to immediate use. We'll also talk about goals versus systems and the roles played by habits and triggers in goal achievement.

Part IV

You'll inevitably fail to achieve some of your goals. Don't be concerned about this. It can happen for a number of reasons, and some may reveal that your time, attention, and focus would be better spent in pursuit of more rewarding ambitions.

Part IV will show you what to do in the event your goals remain unrealized. This is a vital part of the goal-achievement process. It provides valuable feedback on your efforts, and will influence your results whenever you set out to accomplish something down the road.

You now have a roadmap to everything we'll cover in this book. Let's get to work.

PART I

WHY YOU'RE NOT ACHIEVING YOUR GOALS

"A goal properly set is halfway reached." — Zig Ziglar

Creating goals is easy. But if you use the wrong approach, *achieving* them can be almost impossible. It'll certainly make doing so more difficult than necessary.

The goal-setting process *seems* simple: figure out what you want to accomplish and work toward that outcome. The problem is, without a systematic approach, the odds of success are low. The path toward goal achievement is fraught with pitfalls and temptations, and any one of them can derail your efforts.

The good news is that you can easily avoid these hazards. You just need to know what to look for.

In the following pages, we'll examine the seven most common reasons people fail to accomplish what they set out to do. If you've ever been discouraged and frustrated by unrealized goals, there's a good chance you'll find the reasons in this section.

REASON #1: YOU'RE SETTING TOO MANY GOALS FOR YOURSELF

~

The seeming ease of setting goals encourages setting too many of them. This mistake introduces a number of problems. First, you risk stretching yourself too thinly. With only so much time, attention, energy, and capital available to you, some of your ambitions will inevitably get shortchanged.

Second, you risk losing focus on your priorities. Some of your ambitions will naturally be more important to you than others. For example, you may wish to quit smoking, get a promotion at work, and start a workout routine. You might also want to learn to play the guitar, go on an African safari, get your golf game under 90, and write a bestselling novel.

It's fine to have a lot of aspirations. But most of them should go on a *wish list*. Your high-priority goals, the ambitions that are most important to you, should receive more visibility and attention. The fewer there are, the more focused you'll be on accomplishing them.

A third problem with having too many goals is that it inevitably leads to feelings of overwhelm and frustration. Pursuing too many priorities, some of which are bound to conflict, causes stress. With time, burnout will set in, causing you to give up on your plans.

And this leads us to the fourth, and arguably biggest, problem with setting too many goals. You won't make significant progress toward achieving *any* of them. You'll be too distracted, overtaxed, overwhelmed, and frustrated. There's nothing more discouraging than starting with a long list of goals and realizing down the road that you haven't managed to bring any of them to fruition.

Tips For Avoiding Setting Too Many Goals

First, acknowledge that you have limited time to accomplish the things you want to do.

Second, assign a priority (e.g. 1 though 3, A through C, etc.) to each of your goals. Place the top-priority goals on one list. Place everything else on a secondary *wish list*.

Third, look for goals that overlap in some way. Achieving one of them may allow you to work toward another. For example, the desire to stick to a healthy diet and lose weight are complementary goals.

Fourth, focus on the next three months. What do you want to accomplish over this timeframe? Doing this distinguishes your high-priority goals (e.g. start a workout routine) from your "someday" goals (e.g. go on an African safari).

Devoting your limited time, attention, and energy to achieving a small number of *important* goals will dramatically increase your chances of success. In fact, isolating the important ones from the less-important and less-urgent ones is half the battle.

REASON #2: YOU'RE LETTING FEAR DOMINATE YOUR HEADSPACE

~

The brain is a formidable saboteur when it comes to goal achievement. It enjoys routine and complacency, and will go to great lengths to promote both. Striving to achieve goals threatens this comfortable state. The brain fights back in a number of subtle ways to maintain the status quo.

One of these ways is fear. Fear of failure. Fear of success. Fear of the unknown. Fear about presumed weaknesses and shortcomings. Whatever form it takes, it erodes your self-confidence and, if you give it an audience, will eventually convince you to give up.

Have you ever intended to do something - for example, learn to surf, start a side business, or pay off your credit cards - only to decide against trying because you feared the goal was too great a challenge? That was your brain trying to sabotage your plans. It convinced you to underestimate yourself to the point that you resigned yourself to failure.

This predicament establishes a terrible cycle. Fear causes inaction, which leads to failure. Failure reinforces the fear, which discourages taking action. And on and on it goes.

Fortunately, you can break this cycle. With resolve and a bit of self-analysis, you can overcome any fear that's preventing you from working toward your objectives. When you do so, you'll probably discover that the fear you experienced was groundless.

Tips For Purging Fear From Your Headspace

Fear rarely stems from nothingness. There's usually a reason or cause for it. The first step toward overcoming it is to figure out its origin.

For example, have you taken others' undeserved criticism to heart? Were you a target of someone's perfectionism, which made you question your own abilities? Did you suffer a humiliating episode in the past that you've carried with you? While such events are real, the fear that springs from them is usually without merit.

The second step is to reframe the manner in which you perceive success and failure. For example, suppose you want to lose 20 pounds within 90 days. The definitions of success and failure are baked into this particular goal. In three months' time, the numbers will reveal the results with clarity. But you can *expand* the definition of success to include factors that are less dependent on the numbers.

For instance, you can say, "Identify the weight loss tactics that work best for me." Even if you lose fewer than 20 pounds within 90 days, the experience can still be a positive one. You'll have discovered that certain tactics work especially well for you, a success in its own right.

Third, commit to taking action. This advice may sound trite, but it's surprisingly effective. As self-made billionaire and philanthropist W. Clement Stone said, *"Thinking will not overcome fear, but action will."*

Fear will undermine your plans and keep you from moving forward. The most important thing to remember is that it's usually unwarranted. Believe in your abilities. If you struggle with fear, I can almost guarantee you're capable of more than you imagine.

REASON #3: YOU'RE SURROUNDING YOURSELF WITH NEGATIVITY

~

Negativity springs from internal and external sources. Regardless of where ground zero is, it will try to discourage you with defeatist thoughts.

Each of us harbors an inner critic. This critic constantly highlights our faults, filling our heads with self-recriminating thoughts. It's the condemnatory voice that tells us we're not smart enough, good enough, or pretty or handsome enough.

Your inner critic is the mouthpiece of self-doubt.

Adding to this *internal* negativity are the cynical, pessimistic, and judgmental people that surround you. You'll find them at your workplace. You'll see them at your gym. You'll run across them while walking through your neighborhood. They're also among your friends and family members, the people you would normally expect to support your aspirations.

In short, negative people are everywhere.

This presents a problem. Many people claim that others' negativity doesn't affect them. They can simply ignore it. I used to make this claim myself.

But over time, I realized I was wrong. I'm definitely influenced by internal and external negativity. If my inner critic tries to convince me that I'm going to fail, my instinct is to give it an audience. If my friends, coworkers, neighbors, and acquaintances try to discourage me from pursuing a particular outcome, I'm inclined to at least consider their lack of faith and enthusiasm.

In my opinion, most people are like myself in this regard despite claims to the contrary. They're vulnerable to self-doubt. They may not crumble under negativity, but they at least give it an audience, if only for a moment.

The problem is, it sometimes only *takes* a moment for negative thoughts to gain purchase. Once they do, the odds that you'll successfully accomplish what you set out to do plummet.

Tips For Avoiding Internal And External Negativity

Let's start with taming your inner critic. First, examine each accusation to determine whether it's substantiated. For example, suppose your hypercritical inner voice tells you that you're not smart enough to learn a new language.

Unpack this assertion. Is it supported by evidence? Chances are, it's not and you can therefore dismiss it.

Second, recall goals you've achieved in the past. Review past accomplishments. These provide evidence of your capabilities, and will go a long way toward silencing your inner critic.

Third, ask yourself whether this judgmental voice has power over you due to past criticism from others. For example, suppose your parents continuously (and unfairly) berated you for traits they perceived to be faults. Have you carried this criticism with you into adulthood, giving your inner critic more authority in the process?

Now, let's focus on avoiding - or at least minimizing the effect of - the cynical and pessimistic people around you. First, identify them. You'll find that negative people are *typically* negative. They complain and criticize out of habit.

Second, give them less of your time and attention. If given the opportunity, negative people will often monopolize both. Limit your exposure to them. For example, if a coworker begins to complain about something over which neither of you has control, simply say, "I need to get back to work." End the conversation.

Third, ask yourself whether a negative person in your life is motivated to criticize or discourage by negative emotions. For example, suppose you share with a friend that you'd like to write a novel. Your friend, jealous of your ambitions, tells you that you're wasting your time. Once you associate his negativity with jealousy (as opposed to constructive feedback), you can promptly dismiss it as meritless.

Fourth, make connections with positive people. In the same way that negative people can discourage you from taking action, positive people will *encourage* you to do so. Their exuberance and optimism will rub off on you, making you feel as if you can achieve any goal you set for yourself.

REASON #4: YOUR GOALS ARE UNREALISTIC

~

It's good to be ambitious with your goals. Ambition is a vital factor in bettering your life, whether that entails advancing your career, getting married, starting a business, or becoming financially independent. Ambitious goals challenge the status quo, compelling you to step outside your comfort zone to accomplish whatever you aspire to do.

But ambition carries a risk. The eagerness to improve your life may prompt you to set goals that are idealistic and infeasible. That path has only one destination: disappointment.

Unrealistic goals nearly always end in failure. Experiencing this outcome over and over will erode your self-confidence, causing you to question your ability to realize your dreams. With time, you'll avoid setting goals alto-gether, if only to avoid the inevitable letdown and frus-tration.

Why do we set impractical goals for ourselves? One reason is unbridled optimism. We desire to change some-thing about our lives and overestimate our resources, abili-ties, and resilience.

For example, someone who's tired of living a sedentary life decides to start jogging. He sets a goal to jog five miles a day starting *today*. This is an unrealistic goal that's practi-cally guaranteed to end in failure. It's unreasonable to go from couch potato to jogging five miles a day right away, and endure week after week. In this example, the couch potato's enthusiasm to reverse his sedentary life is admirable, but overt optimism sets him up for disap-pointment.

We also set unrealistic goals because we're unclear regarding what's achievable for us. We focus on a desired outcome and resolve to bring it about, but a lack of experi-ence, knowledge, or anecdotal evidence causes us to form misguided expectations.

For example, an individual who struggles with weight management decides to lose 50 pounds. She sets a goal to lose this amount in six weeks. This is an impractical goal. Losing 50 pounds in six weeks is arguably achievable via a crash diet. But such an approach is unhealthy and likely to result in gaining the weight back once the crash diet is abandoned. In this example, the individual's desire to lose excess weight is admirable. But a lack of clarity regarding proper weight loss strategies encourages her to develop and harbor unsound expectations, and ultimately results in disappointment.

Setting challenging goals is commendable. Advisable, even. But it's also important that your goals are *achievable*. Otherwise, you risk experiencing disappointing failure after failure until failure becomes the expected outcome.

Tips For Setting Realistic Goals

First, set milestones for each goal. They'll not only keep you on track, but they'll also validate the sensibility of your goals. For example, suppose you'd like to lose 50 pounds. Commit to losing two pounds per week. This weekly milestone demonstrates the reasonableness of your objective.

Second, write down your goals. This advice sounds pedestrian. But writing down your goals makes them more tangible. You'll be less vulnerable to overt optimism and dubious expectations.

Third, review your available resources. Every goal you set will require time, attention, action, and perhaps even money. Consider whether you possess the resources to bring about your desired outcome. For example, suppose you'd like to save $200,000 in five years. Consider your salary (or the income generated from your business), your monthly expenditures, and taxes. Think about the expected yield on your savings. These factors will determine whether this goal is feasible.

Realistic goals are imperative to your success. They

dictate whether you'll achieve what you set out to do or experience disappointment whenever you try to better your life.

REASON #5: YOU'RE TRYING TO IMPRESS OTHERS

~

For some, the desire to impress others is nothing more than a halfhearted attempt to dazzle people. Whether it succeeds is of nominal importance to the individual. You probably know someone who has a penchant for bragging. He or she seeks to make an impression, but is unlikely to be crushed if his or her audience is unreceptive.

For others, the desire to impress is much more important. It's a desperate bid for validation. Whether or not this bid succeeds is of *great* importance to the individual. It's a form of approval that acknowledges his or her value. To that end, it's an attempt to gain acceptance in another's eyes.

When it comes to setting goals, this tendency to impress people imposes a disturbing side effect. Our aspirations stop being our own, and instead reflect what others want from us. We stop pursuing the betterment of our lives from our own informed, qualified perspectives, and instead strive to meet others' expectations. Worse, we do so regardless of whether those expectations align with the outcomes we desire.

For example, during my first two years in college, I strove to get perfect scores on my exams. The problem was, I wasn't doing so for me. I was doing it to meet the expectations of my parents, professors, and to a limited extent, my friends. I allowed their expectations to dictate my goals.

And I did so to my detriment. I became highly skilled at taking tests, but sacrificed in-depth knowledge of the associated subject matter in the process.

There's another notable downside to setting and pursuing goals with the intent to impress others: we're less *invested* in such goals. We care less about them than we care about the goals that are personal and truly important to us. This alone makes success less likely.

So ask yourself: are you trying to impress people with your goals? If so, now's the time to adjust your frame of mind and focus on goals that align with what *you* want to accomplish.

Tips For Setting Goals That Complement YOUR Ambitions

First, each time you set a goal, gauge whether you've been influenced by others' expectations. It's not necessarily a bad thing if you *have* been so influenced. Others' expectations may align perfectly with what you'd like to accomplish. But whether or not they align, it's crucial that you recognize this influence.

Second, if you notice that one of your goals is designed to impress someone, try to pinpoint the source of your motivation. Why is impressing that person important to you?

There may be a good reason. For example, suppose you'd like to demonstrate your skills and reliability to your boss so she'll reward you with higher-profile projects. But if you *lack* a good reason, reconsider whether the goal is worth pursuing.

Third, make a connection between each goal you set for yourself and the outcome you want to achieve. For example, suppose you decide to lose 50 pounds over the next six months. You might connect this goal with the fact that you'd like to enjoy better health. This outcome is personal to *you*. It reflects what *you* want.

Again, there are practical reasons for setting goals to impress others. But such occasions are the exceptions to the rule. Spend the majority of your time, effort, and focus pursuing goals that complement *your* ambitions.

REASON #6: YOU HAVEN'T GIVEN YOURSELF A COMPELLING "WHY"

∾

Do you ever look back on past goals and wonder why you set them in the first place? They probably seemed important to you at the time, but the reasons escape you in the present.

Such goals are usually abandoned, leaving us to feel disappointed and impotent. Our failure to achieve them wreaks havoc on our self-confidence.

But even success offers little comfort in these circumstances. On the rare occasions we manage to pull off such goals, the sensation of having accomplished something momentous evades us.

We feel empty, as if we've wasted our time.

This problem has a simple root cause. It stems from a lack of purpose. We neglect to give ourselves a powerful reason for accomplishing what we set out to do.

For example, suppose you set out to save $100,000. It's a laudable goal. But without a purpose, it's an empty target. Without a compelling *reason* for saving that sum, you'll be tempted to put your plan on the back burner whenever you're forced to tighten your fiscal belt.

But let's suppose you have a cogent purpose for this goal. For example, you'd like to save $100,000 to give yourself a financial cushion before resigning from your job and starting your own business. Or you'd like to fund your child's college education. Or you intend to use the money as a down payment on your dream home in an idyllic locale.

Purpose is what drives us to take action. Purpose keeps us focused and motivates us to press onward when doing so is difficult. For example, suppose you're tempted to buy a new car, and pay for it outright to avoid interest payments. In the absence of a compelling reason to save $100,000, you'd be inclined to give into the temptation. *With* a compelling reason, it's easier to resist the impulse and stay focused on your true desired outcome.

Tips For Creating Strong "Whys" For Your Goals

Creating a "why" involves making an emotional connection with your goal. These connections will propel you forward when you feel like giving up.

First, think about how accomplishing your objective will make you feel. For example, getting a promotion at your job might make you feel valued and appreciated.

Finding a life partner may make you feel exhilarated and invincible. Saving $100,000 might give you a comforting sense of security.

Second, associate these feelings with your purpose. Connect them. For example, suppose you'd like to lose 30 pounds so you'll look svelte and sexy on an upcoming Caribbean vacation. Looking so will likely make you feel confident and happy. Connect these feelings with your reason for losing the weight.

Third, maintain a gratitude journal. Write down the things for which you're grateful, doing so in the context of each of your goals. For instance, take our example of saving $100,000. You might note your gratitude for having a job that can fund this objective. In our example of losing 30 pounds, you might express your gratitude for the ability (e.g. the use of your limbs) and resources (e.g. the money to pay for a gym membership) you need to accomplish your goal.

A gratitude journal does more than merely focus our attention on things we'd otherwise take for granted. It reminds us that we possess the tools we need to bring about our desired outcomes. It's an exercise in empowerment. Go for depth and don't be afraid to detail the emotional impact of your gratitude.

REASON #7: YOU'RE NOT TAKING ACTION

⁓

Action defines the difference between a goal and a wish. Each goal should come with its own action plan (we'll talk about this in great detail later). The execution of this plan is imperative to success.

By contrast, wishes are merely desires. We've neither made a commitment toward achieving them nor created plans for doing so. Consequently, any effort we make toward bringing about our desires are usually short-lived and abandoned.

This is an important distinction to make. Many people believe they're setting goals when they're actually doing nothing more than identifying their desires. Maintaining a wish list is fine. In fact, I recommend doing so. But a wish list is *not* a goals list. Wishes can *become* goals, but only through planning and execution.

For example, you probably know people who regularly announce their intention to exercise. You've probably also noticed that few ever start. They abandon their intention via inaction. In this scenario, the "goal" is merely a wish. It's unaccompanied by planning and execution.

Now consider the friend who tells you she intends to exercise and becomes committed to the goal. She researches exercises and develops a workout routine. She purchases gym clothes. She creates a reasonable action plan, one that starts slowly and allows her to build momentum over the coming weeks and months.

And then she sticks to her plan. She takes consistent, deliberate action.

These are the "secrets" to goal achievement: planning and execution, topics we'll discuss in great detail in *Part III: My P.R.I.M.E.R. Goal Setting Method*.

Inaction stems from one of two causes (and occasionally both): laziness and overanalysis. Both manifest via procrastination. We delay taking action, promising ourselves and those around us that we'll take action in the future. In most cases, this future point in time never arrives.

Often, we're simply lazy. We're lethargic. Working toward goals requires effort and attention, neither of which we're inclined to invest.

Other times, we overthink the process. We become stuck in the planning stage, and fail to reach the execution stage.

In both cases, our inaction all but guarantees we'll fail

to realize our desired outcomes. Our goals become destined to remain nothing more than wishes.

The good news is, it's easy to get into the habit of taking action. And once you do so, you'll find that following your action plan and accomplishing what you set out to do is a simple step-by-step process.

Tips For Taking Action Toward Achieving Your Goals

First, start with an action plan. It should detail everything you need to do, and when and how often you should do it. Again, we'll tackle this subject later. It's a crucial one and I want to do it justice.

Second, once you've created your action plan, focus on the actions you'll need to take today and tomorrow. Refrain from worrying about the entirety of your plan. Otherwise, you risk becoming overwhelmed, which will sabotage your efforts and cause you to doubt your abilities.

Third, use little pockets of time to take action. The thought of devoting hours at a time is demotivating. Instead, use the 10 to 15 minutes you have available between (and sometimes during) other activities to work toward your goals.

For example, suppose you want to learn to speak a second language. Doing so requires a significant time investment. But you don't *always* need to set aside a large block of time to study. That expectation will only tempt you to procrastinate until "the time is right." Instead, practice your language-speaking skills while waiting in line at

Starbucks, commuting to your job, and between picking up your kids from school and taking them to soccer practice.

The effort you expend during these small time pockets may seem inconsequential. But leveraging these moments will get you into the habit of taking consistent action.

PART II

10 MOST POPULAR GOAL-SETTING SYSTEMS

"Without goals, and plans to reach them, you are like a ship that has set sail with no destination." — Fitzhugh Dodson

There are numerous goal-setting strategies used today by folks who want to improve their personal and professional lives. This section will describe and evaluate those that currently enjoy the greatest popularity.

Some are better than others. And in my opinion, a few do more harm than good. But ultimately, all of them have something valuable to offer, if only insight into the factors that influence success.

The purpose of this section is to scrutinize each of these goal-setting systems, identify their best features, and note their shortcomings. This process will play an important role in the *following* section, where you'll learn the nuts and bolts of my P.R.I.M.E.R. goal setting method. You'll notice that my method simplifies goal setting by incorporating the pivotal features of today's most popular strategies while ignoring their extraneous components.

#1: S.M.A.R.T. GOALS

∽

You may already be familiar with the S.M.A.R.T. system. Let's cover the basics to ensure we're on the same page.

S.M.A.R.T. is an acronym that emphasizes the system's five core tenets:

- S = Specific
- M = Measurable
- A = Attainable
- R = Relevant
- T = Time-Specific

"Specific" means that a goal should have a distinct outcome. For example, it's not enough to aspire to "lose weight." It's better to aspire to "lose 20 pounds." This specificity creates accountability and defines success versus failure.

"Measurable" means that your goal should allow you to monitor your progress. In the example above ("lose 20 pounds"), you can easily track how much weight you've lost by stepping onto a scale once a week and writing down your results.

"Attainable" means that a goal should be realistic. For example, "lose 20 pounds in six months" is feasible for most people. "Lose 20 pounds by next week" is not.

"Relevant" means that a goal should align with your long-term plans and aspirations. This principle dovetails with the idea of "knowing your why," which we covered in *Reason #6* of the previous section (*Why You're Not Achieving Your Goals*).

"Time-specific" means that a goal should be accompanied by a deadline. An example is to "lose 20 pounds by the first day of summer." Having a deadline hones our focus and encourages execution.

I like the S.M.A.R.T. method. It's simple enough to offer clarity and encourage adherence. Meanwhile, it's detailed enough to support creating an action plan.

Having said that, the S.M.A.R.T. goal-setting approach is imperfect. First, there's little attention given to outcomes. Instead, the focus is on tasks and activities. While the "Relevant" part of the S.M.A.R.T. method addresses outcomes, it does so in a manner that's far from comprehensive.

Second, it emphasizes goal achievement over everything else. This aspect may seem beneficial on the surface, but it can do more harm than good. Without awareness regarding how a particular goal fits into your larger plans, it's too easy to become fixated on the short-term feeling of accomplishment.

A third downside to the S.M.A.R.T. approach is that failure to achieve a goal leads to discouragement. After all, a goal that adheres to the five tenets of the approach is achievable. Failure is thus unacceptable. But in reality, failure may simply constitute feedback that a particular goal is no longer important to you. The S.M.A.R.T. system offers little room for self-analysis to that end.

#2: S.M.A.R.T.E.R. GOALS

∿

The S.M.A.R.T.E.R. goal-setting system is an extension of the S.M.A.R.T. system. Two additional tenets are appended to provide a more comprehensive approach. Following is the entire acronym spelled out along with each letter's feature.

- S = Specific
- M = Measurable
- A = Attainable
- R = Relevant
- T = Time-Specific
- E = Evaluate
- R = Revise

You're already acquainted with the first five principles.

The latter two provide greater depth that overcomes some of the shortcomings inherent in the original S.M.A.R.T. method.

"Evaluate" means that a goal needs to be monitored to promote consistent progress. This principle broadens the scope of "Measurable." It's not enough that a goal provides a way to monitor progress (via specificity). There must also be a way to gauge whether changing circumstances affect its achievability.

"Revise" means that a goal should always be open to reassessment. Ambitions and aspirations change with time. Goals must be allowed to change with them. This principle introduces adaption, an indispensable facet, into the goal-setting process. It recognizes that goals can become misaligned with one's long-term plans due to environmental changes, personal obstacles, and other challenges. When this occurs, it allows the individual to realign them.

For example, suppose you set a goal to lose 20 pounds by the first day of summer. You're inspired to look good when you visit the beach or lie poolside to soak up the sun's rays. But let's say you're injured in an auto accident, and your injury prevents you from exercising. Under these circumstances, it may be necessary to revise your goal to accommodate this obstacle.

While I like the S.M.A.R.T. goal-setting system, I feel the S.M.A.R.T.E.R approach is an improvement on the formula. The "Evaluate" step encourages the individual to track his or her progress in a way that's overlooked by the "Measurable" step.

The "Revise" step is an even more important addition. We should continuously ask ourselves whether our goals complement our larger aspirations. Moreover, we should always be receptive to adjusting - or abandoning altogether - goals that fail to meet this standard.

In my opinion, the "Revise" step should be intuitive and instinctive. It's a natural result of an active, dynamic goal-setting approach, and therefore doesn't need to be spelled out. Having said that, because the S.M.A.R.T. and S.M.A.R.T.E.R systems are so meticulous, and those who follow them usually treat them as step-by-step instructions, this step's inclusion is useful here.

#3: OKRS (OBJECTIVES AND KEY RESULTS)

~

The Objectives and Key Results method is simpler than the S.M.A.R.T. and S.M.A.R.T.E.R methods. Here's how it works…

First, set an objective you'd like to achieve. Then, identify the metric that best indicates your progress. Finally, keep your eyes on that metric until you've accomplished your goal.

For example, suppose your objective is to save $20,000. The most important metric (or key result) is the balance in your savings account. Therefore, you'd want to keep your eyes on that number until it reaches $20,000.

OKRs are typically used on an organizational level. For example, a manager might encourage his or her employees to set objectives and identify and track key results to ensure his or her department's goals are achieved. It's an effective way to communicate goals to a large group of people, and align everyone's efforts across the existing hierarchy.

But this approach isn't exclusive to organizations. Many people adopt OKRs in their personal lives, as well. The problem is, on its own, the OKR method is deeply flawed. Its simplicity is its Achilles' heel.

First, it neglects setting deadlines for objectives (recall the "T" in the S.M.A.R.T. and S.M.A.R.T.E.R methods). Without deadlines, there's no sense of urgency prompting action.

Second, it prioritizes the "how" and avoids the "why." That is, the focus is placed on the activities and efforts required to achieve established objectives. No attention is given to whether those objectives should be pursued. They may initially seem important, but as we discussed in the previous section, circumstances change. Our goals must be malleable enough to change with them.

A third shortcoming inherent in the OKR method is that it can cause you to miss opportunities. With so much attention devoted to accomplishing established objectives, and no attention devoted to examining their ongoing merit, you risk misallocating your time, attention, and other resources.

Recall our earlier example of saving $20,000. The OKR approach would have you focused on achieving that objective. But what if you had an opportunity to allocate the money in a way that was better aligned with your longer-term ambitions (for example, investing in a promising stock)? Were you to stick diligently to the OKR method, you'd miss out on such opportunities.

If you decide to experiment with this goal-setting system, I urge you to incorporate the principles of the S.M.A.R.T.E.R method. Specifically, set deadlines and continually reassess the merit of each of your goals.

Better yet, hold off until you've read *Part III: My P.R.I.M.E.R. Goal Setting Method*. It incorporates everything you need to accomplish what you set out to do.

#4: BSQ (BIG, SMALL, QUICK)

~

This approach was invented by David Van Rooy, an expert in organizational psychology. He advocates setting big goals, specifying smaller subgoals that serve as guideposts on the path toward goal achievement, and establishing a timeline.

According to Van Rooy, the first step short circuits our tendency to sell ourselves short. He encourages us to think big, confident that we can accomplish more than we think. The second step establishes a series of benchmarks that can be used to monitor our progress. The third step encourages the use of deadlines to spur us to take action.

For example, suppose you decide to lose 100 pounds. This would represent your "big goal." It may seem impossible, or at least impractical, but we're thinking big.

Next, let's say you intend to lose two pounds a week.

These are your milestones. They represent the smaller subgoals that'll lead you to success.

Finally, suppose you set a timeline of one year. This is your deadline. Assuming that you stick to your goal, you intend to lose 100 pounds by this time next year.

The upside of the Big, Small, and Quick approach is that it encourages us to adopt goals that force us outside our comfort zones. But it's not just an exercise in wish fulfillment. The BSQ method prompts us to create an action plan via milestones. And it spurs us to take action via a deadline.

It promotes both specificity and practicality while offering a way to achieve and gain momentum along the way.

This approach stems from Van Rooy's three core principles of goals:

1. A goal is better than no goal
2. A specific goal is better than a broad goal
3. A hard and specific goal is better than an easy goal

His BSQ system incorporates these three tenets, providing a solid framework that can help us to achieve big results. But it's imperfect. You may have even recognized a few of its shortcomings.

First, like OKRs (see the previous section), it neglects to examine the ongoing merit of our ambitions. No attention is given to re-examination regarding whether our objectives are still important and feasible given changes in our circumstances.

Second, while thinking big and setting big goals is admirable, doing so can also be limiting. Time, attention, energy, and capital are limited resources. Devoting them to achieving a big goal means they're unavailable for other pursuits. This may be fine depending on your focus. But realize that big goals tie up a significant amount of resources.

Third, the BSQ method fails to emphasize task selection with regard to achieving milestones. It's one thing to set guideposts by which to monitor success. It's another thing entirely to identify the actions that must be taken to reach those guideposts. The BSQ approach ignores this step altogether.

Personally, I like Van Rooy's Big, Small, and Quick system. It's simple and concise. But in my opinion, it leaves out important facets of the goal-setting process. These missing components can spell the difference between goal achievement and failure.

#5: THE GOAL BUDDY SYSTEM

∽

This goal-setting system is advocated by the creators of the web-based GoalBuddy program. The details of the program lie beyond the scope of this book. I've never used the GoalBuddy training materials nor mobile app, so I can't speak to their efficacy.

But the GoalBuddy procedure for setting goals is popular enough to profile here. Moreover, it involves organizational elements that I believe are useful for goal achievement.

The system incorporates seven steps. The first step is to reflect on past goals you've successfully achieved. This is intended to give you the confidence you need to accomplish your current and future ambitions.

Second, you're encouraged to imagine how you'd like your life to be in the future, assuming you possessed the necessary resources to make it happen. This is the brain-storming phase.

Third, you're supposed to decide on what you want to accomplish. This step, referred to as a "manifesto" by the GoalBuddy creators, is designed to clarify the output of step two.

Fourth, you're to create an action plan for each goal you highlighted in step three. This step also encourages you to investigate your limiting beliefs, as well as your motivations for each goal.

Fifth, you're to incorporate your action plan into a 90-day timeframe. This step sets a deadline.

The first five steps focus on *setting* goals. Steps six and seven focus on *achieving* them. The sixth step is to find a goal buddy. This person serves as an accountability partner.

The seventh and final step is to regularly meet with your goal buddy - weekly, quarterly, and annually - to review your progress. These meetings extend beyond mere accountability. They're also an opportunity to reassess your goals and resources, and make adjustments as needed.

I admire several components of the GoalBuddy system. For example, I think it's important to imagine your desired life, and then to refine the resulting list of goals according to what you'd truly like to accomplish. I also like that you're prompted to create an action plan for each goal, and then to make each plan time-sensitive. And perhaps most importantly, this approach involves regular reevaluation.

Having said that, it's my opinion that some of the above steps are flawed. For example, while the GoalBuddy system encourages creating a time-sensitive action plan, this time sensitivity is unnecessarily compartmentalized within a 90-day window. This forces the user to focus on each goal for at least 90 days.

The problem is, this is an arbitrary timeline. What if the user decides after two weeks that a particular goal is pointless? Should he or she be compelled to continue devoting resources toward accomplishing it long after it should arguably be abandoned?

Another issue: while I believe it's useful to have an accountability partner, I also feel it's a noncritical step. If the individual is unable to find such a partner, or find a *good* one, it can derail the entire GoalBuddy process.

If you've read any of my other books, you know that I advocate experimentation. To that end, there's nothing wrong with trying the GoalBuddy system and noting whether it produces good results. But I think you'll find my P.R.I.M.E.R. method to be more effective.

6: LOCKE AND LATHAM'S FIVE PRINCIPLES

~

In 1968, Dr. Edwin Locke, a notable psychologist, wrote a paper titled *Toward a Theory of Task Motivation and Incentives*.[1] In this paper, he hypothesized about the effect of specificity in setting goals, as well as various forms of feedback, on performance.

Dr. Locke noted that specific goals lead to better performance than non-specific goals. Moreover, difficult goals lead to better performance than easy goals. And finally, feedback played a crucial role in goal achievement.

He was later joined by Dr. Gary Latham, a professor of organizational effectiveness at the University of Toronto in Canada. Dr. Latham had performed similar research into the factors that influenced task performance. He found similar results. Together, Drs. Locke and Latham came up with five guiding principles of setting effective goals.

Following are these five principles along with a brief explanation of each.

Clarity - This is similar to the "S" in the S.M.A.R.T. and S.M.A.R.T.E.R. goal-setting systems. Locke and Latham assert that creating explicit goals clarifies supporting actions and measuring protocols, and simplifies the identification of success.

Example of a *clear* goal: quit smoking by March 30th.

Example of an *unclear* goal: quit smoking.

Challenge - Locke and Latham maintained that challenging goals motivated individuals and improved their output. As long as a goal was achievable, its difficult nature inspired success. By contrast, easy goals, those that presented little to no challenge, eroded motivation and negatively impacted task performance.

Example of a *challenging* goal: learn to speak German fluently.

Example of an *easy* goal: learn German travel phrases (e.g. "Where's the nearest restroom?").

Commitment - This principle focuses on getting all involved parties on the same page. In a team setting, everyone needs to agree to pursue the goal in question and commit to expending resources (time, focus, capital, etc.) toward its achievement. According to Locke and Latham, this "buy-in" has a positive effect on motivation and improves the likelihood of success.

Commitment is just as important when you're working on your own. Whenever you set a personal goal, it's essential that you're devoted to achieving it.

Example of *commitment*: spending two hours a day, regardless of circumstances, learning to play the guitar.

Example of *non-commitment*: willingness to abandon guitar practice to enjoy other activities (watching TV, meeting friends for dinner, etc.).

Feedback - Locke and Latham claim that monitoring progress plays a crucial role in goal achievement. Being aware of our progress motivates us when our efforts are on track. It also gives us an opportunity to make adjustments as needed.

Example of a *good* feedback loop: weekly reviews to monitor the achievement of subgoal milestones.

Example of a *bad* feedback loop: lack of a regular review process.

Complexity - The complexity of goals has a nominal

impact on performance up to a certain point. Once this point has been reached, it has a severe impact as people begin to feel overwhelmed. Locke and Latham found that overly-complex goals degrade morale and motivation, negatively affecting performance.

Example of *tolerable* complexity: a 5-exercise workout routine that focuses on foundational movement patterns.

Example of *intolerable* complexity: a 20-exercise workout routine optimized with continuously modified sets, reps, and durations.

Locke and Latham's five principles of goal setting hold important keys to success. One example is the emphasis on specificity. The clarity that specificity provides can prove instrumental in creating an effective action plan and monitoring one's progress.

I also like the spotlight on goal complexity. I advocate breaking down processes to their simplest elements because doing so makes them easier to understand. The easier it is to understand the actions we must take to accomplish our goals, the less internal resistance we'll experience while working toward them. And that can only improve our chances of success.

One thing I feel is missing from this goal-setting system is an evaluation of whether specific goals are still meaningful. The principle of feedback is geared toward determining progress. It is not intended to revisit whether our goals continue to hold merit.

This may seem a trivial quibble. But you'll see why it's an indispensable step in *Part III: My P.R.I.M.E.R. Goal Setting Method*.

[1]   HTTPS://WWW.SCIENCEDIRECT.COM/SCIENCE/ARTICLE/ PII/0030507368900044

#7: BACKWARD PLANNING

∿

This approach to setting goals encourages you to start with the outcome you desire and then work backwards to create a plan for achieving it. Backward planning champions the "begin-with-the-end-in-mind" model.

It involves four steps that are designed to produce a feasible, actionable strategy for accomplishing whatever you set out to do. Following are the four steps. I'll use an example of publishing a novel to demonstrate how the system works.

Step 1 - Identify a long-term goal.

Let's suppose you'd like to publish a novel in six months. This is your long-term goal.

Step 2 - Decide on the actions you'll need to take.

Publishing a novel involves numerous tasks. You'll need to write a first draft, proofread it, edit it for clarity, and rewrite the draft, incorporating the changes. You'll need to choose a title, design a cover, format your book, select a price, and plan the release.

You can outsource almost everything (even the writing). The important point is that you highlight the individual measures you'll need to take to accomplish your goal.

Step 3 - Create milestones.

Develop a plan that incorporates each of the measures you identified in the previous step, as well as the deadline you established in the first step. For simplicity, let's focus on the writing aspect of your goal.

A good length for a novel is 80,000 words. Recall that you'd like to publish your novel in six months. You'll likely need a few weeks to edit and revise your first draft. That being the case, let's assume you need to complete your first draft within *five* months.

Five months equals 20 weeks. This means you'll need to write 4,000 words each week, presuming you'd like to avoid scrambling as your deadline approaches. These weekly 4,000-word subgoals represent your milestones.

Step 4 - Go back one step.

Here, we address preliminary measures that should be taken before you start working toward your first milestone.

For example, before you begin writing the first 4,000 words of your novel, you'll need to decide what your novel will be about, create an outline, and choose a book writing software application.

THESE FOUR STEPS encompass the entire backward planning goal-setting system. Simplicity and conciseness are among its charms.

One of the things I like about this approach is its emphasis on developing a sensible action plan. A large goal (publishing a novel) is broken down to smaller, workable subgoals that serve as milestones.

I also appreciate that backward planning encourages the use of deadlines and promotes the identification of necessary measures. These aspects of the system are highly practical.

One of the shortcomings of this approach is that it lacks a formal review process. While milestones keep the individual on track, no attention is given to whether his or her goals continue to have merit.

For example, suppose you decide in the fifth week of writing the first draft of your novel that you intensely dislike writing fiction. In this scenario, it would behoove you to reassess your original goal. Otherwise, you risk spending valuable time and energy on a frustrating pursuit that holds no meaning for you.

In my opinion, this constitutes a significant weakness in the backward planning model. The omission of a review step can precipitate a tremendous waste of time and effort as the individual continues to pursue pointless objectives.

#8: BHAG (BIG, HAIRY, AND AUDACIOUS)

~

This goal-setting approach was popularized by Jim Collins and Jerry Porras in their book *Built To Last: Successful Habits Of Visionary Companies*. While it's typically deployed in an organizational context, it has become increasingly popular among lifestyle management pundits. It dovetails with the idea of setting 10X goals (I'll explain this concept in a few moments).

The basic framework of BHAG is to set a daring long-term goal. This goal is likely to appear extraordinary, even outlandish, to other people. An example would be to aspire to climb Annapurna in Nepal, a mountain that's widely regarded as the most dangerous on Earth. Or to build a billion-dollar company. Or to be elected to the highest public office in the land.

Such goals are considered to be "big, hairy, and audacious."

The steps to creating a BHAG are simple:

Step 1 - Brainstorm a courageous long-term goal.

This goal needs to be big and compelling. It should strike an emotional chord in anyone who hears it. It should also be specific and have a clear destination; there must be no question regarding whether the goal has been achieved.

Step 2 - Evaluate its feasibility.

Ask yourself whether it's truly possible to achieve your goal. Do you have the necessary resources (time, attention, energy, and capital) to make it happen? Can you dedicate these resources over the next several years?

Step 3 - Pledge that you'll achieve your goal.

You commit to doing whatever is necessary to bring about your objective. And the sooner you start taking action, the better.

I MENTIONED above that BHAGs are similar to 10X goals. A 10X goal is a goal that's ten times bigger than what you consider to be practical.

For example, a reasonable goal might be to publish a novel. A *10X goal* would be to publish several novels and watch each one make the New York Times bestseller list.

Is the latter objective doable? Yes. Is it practical? No.

The idea behind setting 10X goals is that failure to reach them can still produce impressive results. For example, you may not see *every* novel you write hit the New York Times bestseller list, but one of them might. And the sales figures of the others might still be spectacular despite their failure to make the list.

BHAGs work in a similar manner. You're encouraged to pick a goal that seems nearly impossible on the surface. But even if you fail to reach it, you'll still benefit from your concentrated efforts. Your efforts are likely to still produce admirable results.

I'll be frank about the BHAG method of setting goals: I dislike it. I feel it omits crucial steps that influence success.

For example, as with backward planning (refer to the previous section), there's no review process. So, there's no formal procedure to determine whether a big, hairy, and audacious goal still has merit. This omission is especially notable given that BHAGs require years of effort.

Another flaw is the lack of a formal step promoting the creation of an action plan. There's an emphasis on making consistent, forward progress, but there's no framework for developing a plan for doing so. Such a step can be *appended* to the BHAG approach, of course. But its absence, even if only at the outset, leaves a notable vacuum.

In my opinion, the BHAG model lacks the finer details that make superior goal-setting systems (e.g. the S.M.A.R.T. and S.M.A.R.T.E.R. methods) effective.

#9: THE GOLDEN CIRCLE METHOD

∾

The Golden Circle approach to goal setting focuses on *why* you want to achieve a particular goal. According to this method, it's only after you determine why that you flesh out the *how* and *what* (in that order).

The idea was conceptualized by Simon Sinek, author of *Start With Why*. In a popular TED talk,[1] Sinek noted that most people focus on *what* they want to accomplish. Some go further and consider *how* they'll accomplish it. But few think about *why* they want to do so.

The Golden Circle method encourages setting goals in the opposite direction. Start with why, then determine how, and finally flesh out the what. Below is an image that illustrates this process.

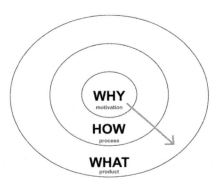

For example, let's suppose you'd like to get into shape. You may be tempted to start with an action plan. But Sinek advocates first determining your reason for getting into shape. What is your motivation? Is it to feel better, sleep better, or reduce your blood pressure? Is it to increase your strength, boost your metabolic rate, or improve your range of motion?

Once you've figured out *why* you want to get into shape, focus on *how* you intend to do it. Will you visit the gym? Will you clean up your diet? Will you abandon unhealthy vices, such as cigarettes and alcohol? This step turns your desire into a practical objective. It lends feasibility to your goal.

Finally, determine *what* you'll need to do to achieve your desired outcome. This is where you create an action plan. If you're focusing on exercise, develop a workout routine. If you're focusing on your diet, design a meal plan. If you're focusing on bad habits, come up with strategies for curbing unhealthy practices.

This framework encourages you to set goals that are

truly important to you, and come up with sensible procedures for achieving them.

I like the simplicity of The Golden Circle. With only three steps, it avoids the unnecessary complexity of other goal-setting methods, preventing us from getting lost in the weeds.

I also appreciate the system's early emphasis on intentionality. I agree with Sinek that it's crucial to be aware of our reasons for pursuing our goals. Our reasons create emotional connections with our desired outcomes. For example, "getting into shape," a goal that, on its own, lacks substance, starts to take form and hold meaning for us.

One of my reservations about The Golden Circle is that it gives little attention to identifying actions that can be measured. The second and third steps (*how* and *what*) promote developing a game plan for achieving a goal, but there's no emphasis on how to do so effectively.

Another shortcoming of this method is that it fails to spur the individual to regularly assess the continuing merit of his or her goals. As we've discussed in prior sections, goals can become less important, or even meaningless, over time. In my opinion, it's vital to identify and abandon such goals as quickly as possible to conserve our limited resources.

The Golden Circle is a good system. But it's imperfect as it omits important steps in the goal-setting process. As always, I encourage you to experiment with different approaches and note how well they work for you. Having

said that, I also encourage you to hold off on this experimentation until you've learned my P.R.I.M.E.R. goal
setting method.

[1]   HTTPS://WWW.TED.COM/TALKS/
SIMON_SINEK_HOW_GREAT_LEADERS_INSPIRE_ACTION

#10: OGSM (OBJECTIVES, GOALS, STRATEGIES, MEASURES)

∾

O GSM is mainly used in organizations. One of its key advantages is that it helps managers to align their goals with the goals of other managers and their respective teams.

This advantage is extraneous to our personal goals. Most of us work towards achieving our personal goals without substantial input from others. So there's no need to organize efforts and allocate resources based on the disparate objectives of multiple parties.

Having said that, the OGSM model offers useful insight.

The system begins with defining a broad objective. Examples would be to "retire," "lose weight," or "travel the world." These objectives should align with your desired life. The alignment gives them meaning.

The next step is to create a list of goals that'll help you to accomplish your objectives. For example, let's say your objective is to retire. To do so, you'll need to have a certain amount of money set aside by a certain point in time. So you'll come up with financial goals, such as *"have $1 million in investments by the time I turn 65."*

Next, the OGSM model prompts you to develop strategies that'll lead to achieving your objectives. This step involves creating an action plan. You identify the actions you'll take to accomplish the goals defined in the previous step, which, in turn, will ultimately fulfill your long-term objective (e.g. retire).

In our example, this might entail investing a specific sum each month into a mutual fund. It may involve reducing your monthly discretionary spending by a certain percentage. It might require evaluating your health care options and adjusting your health insurance plan.

The final step of the OGSM approach is to establish measurable benchmarks. These benchmarks allow you to monitor your progress. They should be specific enough to leave no question regarding whether you're making the progress you envisioned.

Continuing with our "retire" example, let's say you're 45 years old. You have 20 years to accumulate $1 million, presuming you'd like to retire at 65. Estimating a 5% real rate of return,[1] you decide to invest $3,000 a month. You can use an online investment calculator to "map" the amount of money you'll have accumulated by the end of each year leading up to age 65.

If the amount in your investment portfolio matches or exceeds the amount displayed on the map, you'll know that you're hitting your benchmarks. If the amount is lower, you'll know that you need to make compensatory adjustments.

The OGSM method provides a formal process for turning long-term desires into achievable goals supported by realistic milestones. It emphasizes taking measurable actions. This alone distinguishes it from lesser goal-setting systems.

But it has two shortcomings. First, there's no review process during which to assess the ongoing merit of a long-term objective. (As we've seen throughout this section, this is a limitation with many of today's most popular goal-setting systems.) Second, in the absence of a review process, the OGSM model locks you in. Your resources may be consumed for years on end without good reason.

The OGSM model offers useful guidance from a bird's-eye view. But it's far from perfect, and I advise caution if you decide to experiment with it.

[1] REAL RATE of return is the annual return on an investment following adjustments for inflation, taxes, and other external factors.

WHICH IS THE BEST GOAL-SETTING SYSTEM?

~

W e've investigated the 10 most popular approaches to setting goals. So which is the best one?

Simply put, none of them.

As we've seen, each one is flawed. Some are flawed in minor ways. They contain useful building blocks, but are ultimately imperfect. Other systems are flawed in egregious ways that make them entirely unsound.

But most importantly, the "best" system is the one that works for *you*. It does no good to follow an approach that works for other people, but ultimately proves ineffectual in helping you to achieve *your* goals.

With that in mind, I'd like to introduce you to my P.R.I.M.E.R. goal setting method. It addresses the aspects I believe to be the most crucial to accomplishing whatever you set out to do.

It would be hypocritical of me to propose that my method is the best one. That said, I confidently encourage you to try it. I think you'll find that it produces impressive results.

PART III

MY P.R.I.M.E.R. GOAL SETTING METHOD

❧

"Our goals can only be reached through a vehicle of a plan, in which we must fervently believe, and upon which we must vigorously act. There is no other route to success." — Pablo Picasso

❧

My P.R.I.M.E.R. method is an amalgamation of the crème de la crème we covered in *Part II: 10 Most Popular Goal-Setting Systems*. It isolates the best pieces and assembles them into an actionable approach that produces results.

You'll find that my P.R.I.M.E.R. method is a simple system. That's by design. It'll help you to avoid becoming entangled in the trivialities that often accompany setting goals. You'll be better able to focus on the steps that'll truly influence your forward progress and eventual success.

To illustrate the points made throughout this section, I'll use the example of an individual who plans to improve his or her health. Additional examples will be presented to add depth to select concepts, but the "get healthy" example will serve as our constant. The consistency will make it easier to visualize how you'll advance, step by step, through the P.R.I.M.E.R. method whenever you set goals.

Let's dive in.

P - PINPOINT YOUR HIGHEST-PRIORITY AMBITIONS

~

T his step involves self-analysis. It entails contemplating your ambitions and zeroing in on the ones you consider vital to the life you desire to live.

Think of these as your "umbrella" aspirations. They're broad and may involve multiple goals. An example of an umbrella aspiration is to "improve your health." It might be supported by numerous goals such as "eat healthier," "lose weight," "start exercising," "get more sleep," "quit smoking," etc.

To uncover your umbrella aspirations, ask yourself the following two questions:

1. **In what areas of my life would I like to see positive results?** Examples include your

relationships, health, career, finances, attitude,
spirituality, experiences, and
education/knowledge.

2. ***Why* do I wish to see results in these
areas?** Here, you'll isolate the most prominent
motivating factors. These might involve your
core values, such as compassion, honesty, and
personal growth. They may also include feelings
of restlessness (e.g. you desire a more
challenging career), fear (e.g. you want to
improve your health to avoid an early death),
and deeply-held longing (e.g. you desperately
want to travel the world).

Next, we need to differentiate your *critical* umbrella
aspirations from the important, but *expendable* aspirations.
To do so, ask yourself two more questions:

1. **How would I rank my aspirations in
importance?** Each one undoubtedly deserves
your time and attention. Unfortunately, you
only have so much time and attention to
allocate toward them. So write them down and
rank them.

2. **How would I feel if I failed to fulfill
these aspirations?** Some ambitions appear
important on the surface, but seem less so under
close scrutiny. Answering this question gives you
an opportunity to examine how you truly feel

about each one, and determine where your time and attention are best spent.

Your answers to these questions will produce a prioritized list of ambitions. This list is your starting point. It'll influence where you should dedicate your limited resources, and play a crucial role in helping you to create the life (and lifestyle) you enjoy down the road.

If your list contains more than a dozen umbrella aspirations, you'll probably need to abandon a few that are ranked at the bottom. Don't be too concerned that you're doing yourself a disservice. This process will inevitably reveal aspirations that are less important than they initially seem. Upon closer inspection, you'll undoubtedly find they can be abandoned, or at least relegated to the back burner, without serious consequence.

Are Your Ambitions Realistic?

You'll note that none of the above questions address whether your umbrella aspirations are realistic. That's not an oversight. I assume you harbor no delusions. If you're a middle-aged male and weigh 125 pounds, you (hopefully) don't aspire to play in the NFL. If you detest writing and struggle with creativity, you (hopefully) don't aspire to become the next J.K. Rowling.

The more important question is, how do you *know* whether an umbrella aspiration is realistic? Three factors play a role.

First, consider the associated cost. Will it cost time, money, energy, or attentional resources? How much of each? Are you willing to allocate these resources in sufficient volume? For example, suppose you'd like to find a marriage partner, but are unwilling to spend time meeting people. This lack of willingness makes your aspiration to get married unrealistic.

Second, consider existing constraints. Some of them may be related to your resources. For example, suppose you'd like to learn a new language, but your job and home life leave you with no discretionary time. Such a limitation makes learning a new language unrealistic - at least given your current circumstances.

Third, consider external factors over which you have no control. For example, suppose you'd like to visit Yemen. If you live in the U.S., travel to Yemen is prohibited. This circumstance, one you cannot influence, makes visiting Yemen unrealistic.

This step, pinpointing your highest-priority ambitions and determining their feasibility, is one of the simplest in my P.R.I.M.E.R. goal setting method. But it can potentially require the most time and attention. Remember, this is your starting point. It'll affect everything that comes afterward.

R - REFINE YOUR DESIRED OUTCOMES

~

Your list of high-priority ambitions (HPAs) is useful, but only to the extent that you flesh it out with specifics. On the upside, it's comprised of massive, long-term objectives that are important to you. That's helpful because it sharpens your focus. The problem is, unless you refine these objectives with quantifiable outcomes, it'll be difficult to know whether you've achieved them.

For example, suppose you want to improve your health. How do you define success? Avoiding sugary snacks for 24 hours would likely cause a small drop in your blood glucose level, which would technically be an improvement. But does this minor improvement truly constitute success? Does it mean you've satisfied your ambition?

Without measurable outcomes, success is difficult to

recognize. The purpose of this step is to flesh out your HPAs by developing measurable outcomes for each of them. This process is consistent with the "S" and "M" steps ("specific" and "measurable," respectively) from the S.M.A.R.T. and S.M.A.R.T.E.R. goal-setting systems. It also adheres to the "clarity" principle advocated by Locke and Latham's system.

The first step is to identify areas of attention (AOAs) associated with each HPA. Let's use our "get healthy" example to follow this process. We noted in the previous section that this particular HPA might be supported by multiple goals, such as the following:

- eat healthier
- lose weight
- exercise regularly
- get more sleep
- quit smoking

The second step is to think about each AOA in the context of a measurable outcome with respect to your HPA.

For example, we've determined that eating healthier is an important facet of improving your health. We must now break down this AOA to quantifiable specifics. Following are a few ideas:

- eat no more than 2,000 calories per day
- drink no more than 100 calories per day

- restrict sugar consumption to 100 grams
  per day
- limit eating to three meals per day (no snacking)
- limit alcohol to three drinks per week
- eat fish twice each week
- consume 0.8 grams of protein for each
  kilogram of body weight per day

(Note: the above are not my dietary recommendations. They're for illustrative purposes only.)

You now have a way to monitor your progress. Rather than relying on a nebulous objective (i.e. eat healthier), you now possess measurable specifics. You can use them to ensure you stay on track toward achieving your HPA (i.e. improve your health).

The third step is to assign a deadline for incorporating the quantifiable specifics associated with each AOA into your lifestyle. In some cases, it may be possible to make the necessary changes immediately. An example is to eat healthy. Other cases will require unhurried, measured progress.

For example, consider the AOA "quit smoking." While some smokers experience success by quitting cold turkey, others benefit from following a quitting plan. Such plans may include counseling, the use of medications, and integration of coping strategies, all of which support a gradual tapering off of nicotine use.

Deadlines are crucial for these types of AOAs. They inject accountability into the goal-setting process. They also create a sense of urgency. Moreover, they spur us to take action toward achieving our ambitions, allowing us to benefit from momentum and forward progress.

How To Ensure Your Deadlines Are Realistic

Deadlines are only effective if they're pragmatic. If you set impossible deadlines, you'll only guarantee your failure to meet them. Failure after failure will slowly erode your motivation until you lose the will to set goals altogether.

Fortunately, we can avoid this scenario with the help of a little introspection. First, consider all limitations and constraints that might serve as obstacles when incorporating the quantifiable specifics of your AOAs. Take them into account, and plan conservatively.

For example, suppose you intend to exercise regularly as part of your "get healthy" protocol. But let's also suppose that you're 50 pounds overweight, lead a sedentary lifestyle, and struggle with chronic joint pain. These factors will impact your ability to adopt a daily workout routine. It would be foolhardy to set the deadline for exercising daily for the following week. In this scenario, adopting a daily workout regimen might take *several* weeks. Again, plan conservatively.

The second step is to think about what you're willing to sacrifice to embrace the measurable specifics of your AOAs, and how quickly you're willing to do so. It's tempting to race toward goal achievement. But it's sometimes better to take a slow, measured approach.

For example, suppose you're committed to cleaning up your diet. The problem is, you struggle with sugar addiction. Half of your daily caloric intake comes from sweets. In this case, quitting sugar cold turkey is likely to lead to symptoms of withdrawal (mood swings, aches and pains, anxiety, fatigue, etc.). Consider your tolerance for these symptoms when setting your deadline. A longer deadline will allow you to gradually reduce your sugar intake, exposing you to less-pronounced withdrawal symptoms.

Once you've examined your HPAs, brainstormed quantifiable specifics for your AOAs, and set realistic deadlines for the latter, you're ready to create an action plan.

I - IDENTIFY THE ACTIONS YOU'LL NEED TO TAKE

∾

G oals are achieved by taking action. The question is, what actions must you take to achieve your goals?

This stage of the P.R.I.M.E.R. method will reveal them. Along the way, we'll create an action plan you can implement with full confidence that you'll experience success.

Step 1: Determine Every Necessary Task

In the previous two sections, we pinpointed your highest-priority ambitions (HPAs) and identified the relevant areas of attention (AOAs). We then broke the AOAs down to quantifiable specifics.

These details are essential to the goal-achievement

process. They disclose the actions you must take to bring about your desired outcomes. To that end, if you've completed the work in the previous two sections, you've already done the heavy lifting for this step.

Let's go through a quick example. Recall that our umbrella ambition to "get healthy" is supported by the following areas of attention:

- eat healthier
- lose weight
- exercise regularly
- get more sleep
- quit smoking

Let's break down "exercise regularly" to specifics. Following is a sample (note: this is merely for illustrative purposes and shouldn't be taken as my recommended workout routine):

- exercise four times per week
- perform pushups
- perform squats
- perform planks
- perform jumping jacks
- perform bicep curls with dumbbells

These are the actions that'll satisfy this particular area of attention. Note how going through this process does the heavy lifting (no pun intended) for you with regard to completing this first step.

You'll probably need to add a few items to flesh out your list. For example, commit to exercising on the same four days each week. Also, commit to exercising at the same times on each of the four days. You may also want to add the following to your list:

- recruit an exercise partner for accountability and motivation
- maintain an exercise log that you can use to monitor your progress
- set out your workout gear the night before to reduce resistance

These actions support consistency. As they become part of your normal routine, you'll experience less internal friction.

Write them down. Don't rely on your memory. Writing them down will boost your continual awareness of them and help you to focus when your brain tries to distract you with temptations that offer swift gratification.

Step 2: Establish Milestones

Now that we've identified the necessary actions, we can develop an action plan. In the previous section, *R - Refine Your Desired Outcomes*, we talked about the value of setting deadlines for your AOAs. Deadlines generate urgency, which promotes taking action. This element is crucial to creating momentum that leads to goal achievement.

In this step, we'll work backwards from our deadlines to develop a series of milestones. These milestones will ensure that we're making forward progress at an acceptable pace.

Let's suppose, as part of our "get healthy" protocol, we want to perform the following workout within three months.

- 50 pushups
- 40 squats
- three 60-second planks
- 100 jumping jacks
- five sets of 10 bicep curls (with dumbbells)

Three months is the deadline. Now, let's work backwards to create milestones. Following is a workout routine you might aspire to perform at the beginning of week nine:

- 40 pushups
- 30 squats
- three 40-second planks
- 75 jumping jacks
- five sets of seven bicep curls

Here's a routine you might aspire to perform at the beginning of week six:

- 30 pushups

- 20 squats
- three 30-second planks
- 50 jumping jacks
- five sets of five bicep curls

Continuing to work backwards, here's a hypothetical routine for the beginning of week three:

- 20 pushups
- 10 squats
- three 20-second planks
- 25 jumping jacks
- three sets of five bicep curls

And following is the workout routine we'll start with:

- 10 pushups
- five squats
- three 10-second planks
- 15 jumping jacks
- two sets of five bicep curls

Each of these routines represent a set of milestones. At any point during the next three months, you'll be able to note immediately whether your efforts to "exercise regularly" are going according to plan. And importantly, you'll be able to tell whether you're on track to meet your deadline.

These two steps, determining necessary tasks and

creating milestones, are essential for developing an action plan. They work in tandem, each one supporting the other.

Once you've developed an action plan for each area of attention, you'll have the components of a grander, comprehensive action plan that'll help you to realize your high-priority ambition.

But we're far from done. You'll need to take further steps to guarantee your success. One of those steps involves your environment.

M - MODIFY YOUR ENVIRONMENT TO COMPLEMENT YOUR GOALS

~

Environmental factors are commonly overlooked when setting goals. Many people take great care in identifying their goals and creating plans of action, but neglect to consider the impact of their immediate surroundings.

Your environment can help you accomplish whatever you set out to do. Or it can sabotage you. The good news is, you can influence your environment so that it does the former.

For example, suppose you're trying to concentrate on a task that demands your full attention. If you're at home and your family is creating a lot of noise, you can take shelter in a quiet room. If you're at the office and coworkers keep dropping by to chat, you can ask them to desist until you've finished your work. Doing so is an example of modifying your surroundings to complement your goal.

There are two ways to approach this stage of my P.R.I.M.E.R. goal setting method. The first way is to implement your action plan and react when obstacles surface and threaten to sabotage you.

The second way is to be proactive. Rather than reacting to detrimental circumstances, you take the initiative by identifying environmental factors that might pose a problem. Then, you shape your environment to sidestep them.

This is the strategy I recommend.

This stage consists of two steps. Neither of the steps is difficult. But both can greatly influence the choices you make, which will ultimately decide between goal achievement and failure.

Step 1 - Single Out Potential Environmental Obstacles

Environmental obstacles to goal achievement come in two major forms: distractions and temptations. Some obstacles can take both forms.

Contemplate potential stumbling blocks for each area of attention you defined as supportive of your high-priority ambition.

Let's return to our "get healthy" example. Recall that we identified "eating healthier" as an area of attention relevant to this HPA. Let's think about environmental factors that may distract or tempt us from sticking to a healthy diet. Following are a few ideas:

- junk food in the kitchen pantry
- lack of healthy snacks at home
- sugar addiction
- special social occasions
- too-large portion sizes at mealtimes
- lack of cooking equipment
- friends who discourage us (e.g. *"Don't be a stick in the mud. Have some cake and ice cream."*)

There are, of course, many other potential distractions and temptations, but you get the idea. Once we've identified these environmental obstacles, we can address them in a reasonable manner.

Step 2 - Brainstorm Compensatory Measures

In this step, we'll examine each environmental obstacle and come up with a practical way to manage it. Doing so gives us the tools we need to overcome challenges without being deflected from our goals when such challenges rear their heads. We're essentially planning for potential hazards to minimize their future impact.

Let's go through each of the environmental factors singled out above. I'll present each one below and propose a compensatory measure to resolve it.

Problem: junk food in the kitchen pantry
Solution: discard all junk food immediately

Problem: lack of healthy snacks at home
Solution: fill your kitchen with healthy snack foods (e.g. almonds, hard-boiled eggs, beef jerky, etc.)

Problem: sugar addiction
Solution: abstain from all sweet-tasting foods and beverages

Problem: special social occasions
Solution: eat a healthy meal before you arrive at a get-together

Problem: too-large portion sizes at mealtimes
Solution: immediately reduce portion sizes by 25%

Problem: lack of cooking equipment
Solution: purchase basic kitchen tools (e.g. chef's knife, tongs, colander, frying pan, sauce pan, slow cooker, cutting board, etc.)

Problem: friends who discourage us (e.g. *"Don't be such a stick in the mud."*)
Solution: ask your friends to respect your dietary choices

There's no way to eradicate all distractions and temptations that threaten to sabotage you. But if you plan for them, you can respond to them quickly, sensibly, and decisively without disrupting your momentum.

And that ensures you'll make consistent, forward progress toward achieving your goals.

E - EVALUATE YOUR PROGRESS

∽

Every step of the P.R.I.M.E.R. goal setting method is important. But *this* step is absolutely pivotal to your success. You must monitor your progress. Otherwise, you cannot know for certain whether you're on track to accomplish what you set out to do by your chosen deadline.

The good news is, this step is easy. You've already done most of the work in previous steps:

- you've pinpointed your highest-priority ambitions (HPAs).
- you've identified the relevant areas of attention (AOAs).
- you've broken down your AOAs into goals, each accompanied by quantifiable specifics.

- you've established feasible deadlines.
- you've created an action plan composed of milestones.

Evaluating your progress is a simple matter of performing a periodic review. This practice will not only ensure you're on track to achieve your goal, but will also give you confidence and motivate you to continue.

How To Track Your Progress

We assigned quantifiable specifics to each AOA because numbers are more precise, and thus easier to track, than qualitative factors.

For example, recall that we identified "losing weight" as an area of attention relevant to our ambition to "get healthy." A quantitative approach would allow us to easily observe our progress and note whether we're on track. If our action plan consisted of losing two pounds per week, evaluating our progress would be a simple matter of watching this number.

A *qualitative* approach complicates this process. Without the precision of data, we're left to evaluate our progress based on unreliable factors. Such factors include how we appear, how our clothes fit, and whether other people compliment us.

So, the first step to evaluating whether you're on track is to record facts and figures along the way. For example, if your goal is to lose weight, step on a scale each day and record the resulting number. If your goal is to save $100,000, record the sum and date of each deposit (or investment). If your goal is to perform 100 pushups per day, write down how many pushups you do each time you exercise.

Next, compare these numbers to your predefined milestones to note whether you're making headway that's consistent with your action plan. This is done via the second step: conducting a periodic review.

How To Perform A Periodic Review

Each review session allows you to note your progress, acknowledge your momentum, and ponder the feasibility of your milestones in the event you're failing to reach them. And most importantly, each session gives you an opportunity to make adjustments as needed.

I recommend conducting *weekly* review sessions. Doing so will help you to form the habit. The sessions will eventually become part of your weekly routine, making them feel less like a chore.

Step 1

Choose a specific day of the week, and time of the day, to perform your review. This will further ingrain the habit into your weekly routine. I do my reviews on Sunday evenings (7:00 p.m.). You might prefer Tuesdays at 10:00 a.m. or favor Fridays at 3:00 p.m. Select a day and time that complement your work schedule, home responsibilities, and lifestyle.

Step 2

Choose a place to perform your review. While you can evaluate your progress in any location, the consistency of doing it in the same place each week further sets the habit. I used to conduct my weekly reviews at Starbucks because I enjoyed the change of scenery. These days, I conduct them in my home office because I favor the privacy and quietude.

Step 3

Create a simple agenda to guide your review sessions. This agenda should include a small checklist along with a few probing questions, all of which are designed to help you appraise your progress during the previous week.

Following is an example checklist for the goal of losing weight. Note that some of the items are taken from the environmental obstacles we identified in the section *M - Modify Your Environment To Complement Your Goals*:

- Achieved weekly milestone
- Avoided buying sugary snacks
- Had healthy snacks on hand
- Ate smaller portion sizes
- Abstained from sweet foods and beverages

Following is a list of example probing questions:

- Did I have sufficient energy?
- Did I feel physically exhausted?
- Was I able to focus on my work?
- How much internal resistance did I experience?
- What did I do well?
- What could I do better?
- Did I face any unanticipated obstacles?

Once you've created your agenda, use it each week. If you come up with additional checklist items and questions that would prove beneficial to your weekly review, feel free to add them. This is *your* template. Modify it according to your circumstances.

Step 4

The final step is to look forward rather than backward. After you evaluate your progress during the previous week, consider the following week. Review your checklist and questions in the context of what you anticipate over the next seven days.

This step reinforces your expectations. It also prepares your mind to overcome any internal friction you might experience. For example, you'll be more inclined to avoid sugary snacks during the coming week if you reflect on the fact that it's important enough to be on your checklist.

Evaluating your progress may seem like a complicated

process. But remember, you've already done most of the work in previous stages of the P.R.I.M.E.R. goal setting method. Once you create a simple agenda, you're well on your way.

Your weekly review sessions will likely take no more than 15 minutes. And after it becomes a habit, a normal part of your weekly routine, it'll seem like hardly any work at all. If you're like me, you'll even look forward to the process.

R - REVISIT YOUR GOALS

$\sim$

You'll recall that I highlighted the absence of this step in many of today's most popular goal-setting systems. I consider that omission to be a significant shortcoming. Below, I'll explain two reasons.

Reason #1: Loss Of Relevance

Many goals lose relevance over time. They become less important to us as our lives progress. When this occurs, it's in our interest to abandon them, or at least put them on the back burner. Otherwise, we risk wasting limiting resources trying to achieve ambitions that are no longer meaningful to us.

For example, suppose you're dissatisfied with your job

and decide to quit and start your own business. You set a goal to save 12 months of living expenses to provide a financial cushion. Over the next few months, you save every penny you can for this purpose.

One day, your boss calls you into her office. She promotes you to a highly-coveted position, one you've desired for years. The promotion causes your dissatisfaction to evaporate, and you no longer entertain the idea of quitting.

In this scenario, your goal of saving 12 months of living expenses has suddenly become less important. It's still a worthwhile goal, but you no longer have a sense of urgency stemming from your plans to quit your job and start a business. Revisiting this goal gives you an opportunity to decide whether to abandon it, freeing your attention for more important pursuits.

Reason #2: Loss Of Feasibility

Some goals become infeasible due to prevailing circumstances. When this occurs, it's in our interest to identify the challenges and decide whether to adjust our plans or relinquish the goals altogether. Otherwise, we risk wasting limited resources with no hope of success.

For example, suppose you decide to adopt a healthy diet. A crucial factor in achieving this goal is cooking your own meals. To that end, you furnish your kitchen with basic cooking tools and stock your refrigerator with natural foods. You also create an action plan, complete with weekly milestones, that you intend to execute immediately.

One day, your boss calls you into her office. She informs you that you must visit several clients over the next few weeks. You'll be on the road during this time.

In this scenario, cooking your own meals over the next few weeks will no longer be feasible. You'll need to revisit your goal and adjust your action plan to accommodate the change in your circumstances.

When To Revisit Your Goals

The best time to decide whether your goals are still important and feasible is during your weekly reviews sessions. It's a natural fit.

If you discover that you're failing to achieve your weekly milestones, you'll already be inclined to investigate the reasons. You may discover that your circumstances have made the goal in question, along with its accompanying milestones, less practical. In such cases, it's necessary to make changes.

Even if you're achieving your milestones, this is still an ideal time to consider whether the goal in question is still a priority for you. You might find that, despite your success, you're pursuing an ambition that is no longer relevant given your circumstances.

There's no dishonor in abandoning goals that are no longer important, feasible, or even beneficial. In fact, doing so is highly advisable. It frees up resources you can then devote to more momentous aspirations.

In my opinion, this is a critical step in the goal-achievement process. Any system that ignores it is suspect.

GOALS VERSUS SYSTEMS: WHICH SHOULD YOU FOCUS ON?

66 By recording your dreams and goals on paper, you set in motion the process of becoming the person you most want to be. Put your future in good hands—your own." — Mark Victor Hansen

GOAL SETTING HAS EXPERIENCED a minor backlash over the last several years. Critics note that setting goals seldom influences behavior, which is the reason so many people fail to accomplish what they set out to do.

For example, consider people who announce they intend to start exercising at the beginning of the year. It's a common New Year's resolution. And true to their intentions, when January arrives, they join a gym. They hit the machines a few times each week, enthused about making a positive change in their lives.

This goes on for a few weeks until the visits taper off. By February, most of these folks have stopped going altogether.

What went wrong?

One school of thought critical to the practice of setting goals claims the problem is that people are forced to rely on personal grit. When the going gets tough, or when more appealing activities compete for their attention, they predictably abandon their goals.

Detractors advocate developing *routines* instead of goals. The reasoning goes something like this: routines encourage habits. And according to these critics, habits are more important than goals because the former are more likely to lead to long-term behavioral change.

They're correct, at least partially so.

Developing routines does indeed encourage developing good habits. Moreover, once such habits become ingrained in our heads, they influence our behavior. They eventually become part of our normal processes to the point that we don't need to rely on grit for them to happen.

For example, consider the practice of brushing your teeth before going to bed each evening. It requires little thought or discipline. It happens because it's part of your nightly routine. The result is good dental health.

So habits and routines are important. Crucially so, in fact. But neither negate the value of setting goals.

The reason so many people fail to accomplish what they set out to do is found in the goal-setting process. The first problem is that they set goals that are either infeasible or unimportant. They either lack the resources to achieve them or are less emotionally invested in their goals than they imagine.

The second problem is the lack of an action plan. They neglect to break down their goals to subgoals accompanied by quantifiable milestones and deadlines.

The third problem is excess rigidity. Once a goal has been set, little thought is given to whether it continues to make sense as circumstances change.

These three problems predictably lead to failure. The good news is that all three can be easily avoided when you use my P.R.I.M.E.R. goal setting method.

In my opinion, there's no reason to choose routines over goals, or vice versa. We benefit from both. Here's the best news of all: if you use my P.R.I.M.E.R. method, you'll find that you *naturally* develop the habits and rituals you need to achieve the goals you set.

That process is baked into the system.

Goals, Habits, And Triggers: The Success Trifecta

At this point, you're a bona fide expert on goals. You know how to set them. And you know how to bring them to fruition. You know the steps involved, and the order in which to take them.

Let's focus on habits and triggers, and connect them to

specific steps of the P.R.I.M.E.R. goal setting method. Specifically, we'll focus on the "I" and "M" parts of the method.

In the section "*I - Identify The Actions You'll Need To Take*," we discussed creating a game plan for each goal. A core piece of the process was to highlight every relevant area of attention (AOA). Recall that our umbrella ambition to "get healthy" included the following AOAs:

- eat healthier
- lose weight
- exercise regularly
- get more sleep
- quit smoking

We then broke down the AOA "exercise regularly" to the following actions:

- exercise four times per week
- perform pushups
- perform squats
- perform planks
- perform jumping jacks
- perform bicep curls with dumbbells

Then, we created a list of goals associated with these tasks, all of which we intended to achieve within three months:

- 50 pushups
- 40 squats
- three 60-second planks
- 100 jumping jacks
- five sets of 10 bicep curls (with dumbbells)

Finally, we developed an action plan, along with milestones, for each task. Following is the plan we created for pushups:

- Week 1: 10 pushups
- Week 3: 20 pushups
- Week 6: 30 pushups
- Week 9: 40 pushups
- Week 12: 50 pushups

If you were to stick to this plan, you would develop the habit of doing pushups as a natural effect of the goal-achievement process. Doing pushups would become a part of your routine. By the end of the third month, your inclination to do them would be less reliant on discipline and *more* reliant on ritual (similar to brushing your teeth before going to bed).

This is how the "I" in the P.R.I.M.E.R. goal setting method *naturally* leads to good habits that support your ambitions.

Now, let's consider triggers. Every habit is connected to at least one. Triggers are cues that prompt habitual behaviors, both positive and negative, healthy and unhealthy. For example, spending time with certain friends might prompt you to smoke. Or you may be conditioned to visit the vending machine at your workplace at 10:00 a.m. Or boredom might prompt you to immediately check Facebook.

Many triggers are inherent to our environment. This is good news because we can influence our environment, removing some triggers and implementing others as our needs dictate.

In the section *"M - Modify Your Environment To Complement Your Goals,"* we talked about identifying environmental obstacles that could sabotage our intentions. We also discussed coming up with compensatory measures for dealing with them.

Recall that one of the obstacles we identified for our AOA "eating healthier" was the presence of junk food in the kitchen pantry. Also recall that the prescribed solution was to "discard all junk food immediately."

How does this process affect your triggers? Suppose stress is a cue for you. When you feel stressed, you instinctively reach for junk food. By removing such foods from your home, you short-circuit this trigger, severing its effect on you.

The absence of healthy snacks was also identified as a potential environmental obstacle to "eating healthier." We came up with the solution to "fill your kitchen with healthy snack foods." Here, we can *create* a trigger. Whenever you feel stressed, reach for almonds, hard-boiled eggs, or beef jerky. Over time, your mind will become conditioned to do so.

This is how the "M" in the P.R.I.M.E.R. goal setting method *naturally* addresses cues and habitual behaviors. And importantly, it does so in a way that aligns with goal achievement.

Final Thoughts On Goals Versus Systems

Both are vital to accomplishing whatever you set out to do. Moreover, they can be highly symbiotic. A proper goal-setting approach will naturally establish routines and habits that improve your odds of success.

PART IV

WHAT TO DO IF YOU FAIL TO ACHIEVE A GOAL

~

"Every adversity, every failure, every heartache carries with it the seed of an equal or greater benefit." – Napoleon Hill

"Some failure in life is inevitable. It is impossible to live without failing at something, unless you live so cautiously that you might as well not have lived at all -- in which case, you fail by default." - J.K. Rowling

~

Failing to accomplish a goal leaves an empty feeling. It's a troubling and off-putting sensation. Worse, it gives voice to our inner critics, which nag us and point to our failure as evidence of our inadequacy. This negativity, if left unchecked, can sap our motivation and discourage us from striving to improve our lives.

Here's the good news: these negative feelings can be eradicated by taking a clinical approach to investigating the cause of the failure. There are many reasons we might fail to achieve our goals. And nearly all of them point to factors that have *nothing* to do with personal inadequacies.

This section will take you, step by step, through an objective process of evaluating unrealized goals. Along the way, remember that failure to accomplish something is nothing more than feedback that things didn't work out according to our plans.

Our focus here is to figure out why.

PERFORM A GOAL AUTOPSY

∽

When someone dies and there's uncertainty regarding the cause of death, a pathologist performs an autopsy. The purpose of the procedure is to figure out why the individual died. Was it due to injury? Was it due to disease? How healthy was the individual prior to his or her death, and what events (e.g. diagnosis and treatment) preceded it?

There's no emotion involved in this process. It's an investigation, one that sometimes reveals unknown circumstances, the avoidance of which may have prevented the person's demise.

When you're faced with goal failure, it's important to take this approach to figure out the reasons. Rather than accepting the failure at face value, and in doing so giving your inner critic license to condemn you, investigate the matter. You're sure to learn something insightful you can use to your benefit when setting goals in the future.

So, how do you perform a goal autopsy? The following sections will walk you through the most important steps.

Before you proceed, commit yourself to figuring out what went wrong. Make this objective your top priority. The details revealed during this goal autopsy may be unpleasant as they'll highlight apparent weaknesses. But if you focus on the investigation, and remain clinical throughout the process, you'll be better able to use the information to your advantage down the road.

DETERMINE THE ROOT CAUSE OF THE FAILURE

~

G oal failure often stems from multiple causes. But there's usually *one* contributing factor that gives rise to the others. This is the root cause.

In many cases, it's camouflaged by circumstances and psychological blind spots. Our objective in performing this goal autopsy is to find it, examine it, and learn from it. This procedure will reveal other causes that stem from the *root* cause, providing a comprehensive picture of why we failed to accomplish what we set out to do.

We'll use our previous goal to "exercise regularly" (part of our "get healthy" protocol) to illustrate this process.

Step 1: Define The Problem

This step may sound unnecessary, but it's worth doing nonetheless. There's value in expressing, with specificity, the essence of our failure.

Recall that our goal was to perform the following exercises several times per week within three months' time:

- 50 pushups
- 40 squats
- three 60-second planks
- 100 jumping jacks
- five sets of 10 bicep curls (with dumbbells)

Let's assume we failed to do so. To that end, we define the failure as such: *at the end of three months, we are not consistently performing the exercises as planned.*

With the problem clearly stated, we can begin the investigation in earnest.

Step 2: Identify All Potential Causal Factors

As noted above, many reasons might contribute to our failure. The problem is, unless they're listed plainly in front of us, some may remain hidden. And if we're unaware of them, there's nothing we can do to resolve them.

With that in mind, let's brainstorm every possible factor that may have played a role in our failure to "exercise regularly." It's important to be thorough, even to the extent that some of the listed factors had a nominal effect on the outcome. Following are several possibilities:

- lack of energy
- lack of time
- lack of motivation
- lack of workout clothes
- stress
- boredom during exercise
- discouragement from lack of progress
- burnout
- soreness
- no transportation to gym
- can't afford gym membership
- didn't know how to use gym equipment
- action plan was too aggressive
- no accountability partner
- often distracted by more gratifying activities
- negative self-talk
- lack of support from spouse, friends, and family members

There are, of course, many other possible factors. But the above list will suffice for our purposes. Let's assume it's exhaustive so we can proceed with our hypothetical investigation.

Step 3: Determine A Proximate Causal Chain For Each Factor

This sounds complicated. But it's simple, although it requires a bit of time. We're going to take each of the causal factors identified in step two, and work backwards to identify events and conditions that may have led to it.

Let's use "lack of energy" as an example. Upon closer scrutiny, we determine that it was indeed a major culprit that played a significant role in our failure. So let's brainstorm potential reasons for our fatigue:

- lack of quality sleep
- poor diet
- dehydration
- anemia
- depression
- thyroid disorder
- emotional stress

Let's continue by building a proximate causal chain for "lack of quality sleep," the first item on the above list. Following are potential causes:

- stay up too late in the evening
- wake up too early in the morning
- poor diet
- depression
- stress and anxiety

- alcohol consumption
- select medications
- environmental noise (e.g. spouse's snoring, loud neighbors, etc.)

Let's assume that our lack of quality sleep is mainly due to "staying up too late in the evening." So let's work backwards from that particular causal factor. (Normally, we'd go through this process for each of the listed items. But for the sake of timeliness, we'll do so for this item alone.) Following are possible reasons we stay up late:

- watch a favorite television program
- work on an important project
- surfing the internet
- enjoy "me" time (e.g. quiet, solitude, etc.)
- fear of missing out

We can probably work backwards even further. But let's stop here. Let's assume that we stay up too late in the evening because we watch episode after episode of our favorite TV program on Netflix.

We've just completed a simple root cause analysis. Importantly, we now know what to change to resolve the bigger issue.

If we change our Netflix-viewing behavior, we'll go to bed earlier. If we go to bed earlier, we'll get more sleep. If we get more sleep, we'll have more energy. And finally, if we have more energy, we'll be more inclined to exercise on a regular basis. Specifically, we'll be inclined to exercise according to the action plan we created to keep us on track toward achieving our goal at the end of three months.

Root cause analysis only *sounds* daunting. The fact is, it's easy. More importantly, it'll reveal the true reasons you had difficulty accomplishing a particular goal.

And *that* intel will prove invaluable as you set new goals.

REASSESS THE GOAL'S IMPORTANCE TO YOU

~

Back when I was a kid, I'd regularly ask my mother for money to buy a Slurpee® at the local 7-Eleven. My mother, always averse to giving into such pleas, would offer me a deal. If I agreed to pull the weeds in the backyard, dust the furniture in the house, or water the plants outside, she'd happily give me the money.

In other words, I had to work for it.

Of course, I'd use every rhetorical tactic at my disposal to try to persuade my mother to give me the cash immediately. But it was never to any avail. She would always respond by saying, *"If you want the Slurpee® badly enough, you'll do what's necessary to earn it."*

Frankly, I hated hearing those words as a child. But today, I recognize the inherent wisdom. And the lesson has stuck with me for nearly half a century. I think about it whenever I fail to achieve one of my goals.

How badly did I want to accomplish what I set out to do? How important was it to me? And if I decide to once again pursue it, what am I willing to sacrifice to achieve it?

These are crucial questions to ask ourselves in the face of goal failure. We may dislike the answers. After all, they reveal a fatal misalignment between our desires, priorities, and intentions. But the brutal honesty that stems from asking these questions has enormous value.

First, it identifies ambitions that are less significant than we originally imagined. That gives us permission to abandon them so we can devote our limited resources toward more rewarding pursuits.

Second, it allows us to realign our ambitions with our priorities. It gives us an opportunity to recognize the cost of achieving the failed goal, and deciding whether we're willing to pay that cost. Oftentimes, we underestimate the cost in terms of time, attention, energy, and capital, even when we're armed with a practical action plan. Reevaluating a failed goal's importance gives us a chance to adjust our cost expectations, and decide whether or not to pursue it accordingly.

REVISIT YOUR "WHY"

～

I n the section *Reason #6: You Haven't Given Yourself A Compelling "WHY,"* we talked about the importance of having a powerful reason for achieving each goal. A powerful reason gives us purpose. This purpose drives us to take action.

Consider our "get healthy" example from earlier. Suppose your doctor told you that your current lifestyle (i.e. no exercise, poor diet, excess weight, lack of sleep, and habitual smoking) was putting significant strain on your heart. Let's also suppose your doctor said that without serious lifestyle changes, your quality of life would plummet in the coming years.

This is a powerful reason to pursue better health. If you took your doctor's warning seriously, and genuinely feared a substantial decline in your quality of life, you would almost certainly achieve your goal.

But let's say you had received no such news from your doctor. As far as you know, you're in relatively good shape even though you lead a sedentary lifestyle and maintain several unhealthy vices. Your original motivation to "get healthy" was prompted by a vague desire to appear more attractive.

This is *not* a powerful reason. At least not to the extent that it'll prompt you to take action when you experience resistance. For example, let's say you aspire to exercise daily in pursuit of better health. You'd be inclined to forgo exercise whenever you're distracted by more gratifying activities (e.g. sitting on the couch and watching Netflix). After all, the desire to "look better" carries no urgency.

This is the reason it's important to revisit your "why" whenever you fail to achieve a goal. It's possible that your original "why" wasn't sufficiently compelling. Or perhaps it *was* compelling, but your circumstances have changed, making it decidedly less so.

There's no dishonor in failing to accomplish something you have no reason or desire to pursue. On the contrary, recognizing the goal failure in this light is empowering. It allows you to refine your focus and devote yourself to ambitions for which you feel a truer sense of urgency and consequence.

DO A RESET

~

What if you fail to achieve a particular goal, and you decide the goal is still important to you? What should you do in such a case?

If you've conducted a root cause analysis as described in the section *Determine The Root Cause Of The Failure*, you've identified the problematic factors. That means you can adjust your process to prevent them from sabotaging you going forward.

Such adjustments might entail forming new habits that better support your ambitions. For example, suppose you determine a lack of energy is preventing you from exercising. During a root cause analysis, you discover that a poor diet is the culprit. In this scenario, you'd want to form a habit of eating nutritious foods.

Adjustments might also entail curbing old habits that

hamper your progress. For example, suppose your lack of energy is due to poor-quality sleep, which, in turn, is caused by alcohol consumption in the evening. Here, you'd want to curb such alcohol consumption.

You may also need to adjust your action plan. It's possible the plan you've created, along with its milestones and deadlines, is overly-aggressive. If that's the case, you'll need to alter the plan to make it more realistic according to your circumstances.

Remember, goal failure is merely feedback. It doesn't define your worth. It simply indicates that your plan isn't working as you imagined, and provides the impetus to investigate the reasons. Assuming your goal is still important to you, and you're willing to pay the costs associated with achieving it, this is an opportunity to do a reset.

And a new plan with minor adjustments, combined with a compelling "why" and a renewed commitment to success, can hold the key to accomplishing whatever you set out to do.

FINAL THOUGHTS ON THE P.R.I.M.E.R. GOAL SETTING METHOD

∼

S etting goals seems a simple practice, at least on the surface. And with the right approach, it definitely *can* be. The problem is, with so many goal-setting systems currently in use, it's difficult to know which one holds the greatest promise.

Choosing the right method is a pivotal matter as the *wrong* method can cripple your efforts.

The purpose of this book was to introduce you to the system that has worked for me over the years. I credit the P.R.I.M.E.R. method for the majority of my successes with respect to setting and achieving goals. It's a recipe I developed by cherrypicking the most important ingredients found in other goal-setting systems, and leaving the rest behind. I've found it to be very effective.

Is my P.R.I.M.E.R. goal setting method the ideal

approach for everyone? I'll be the first to say no. Each of us responds uniquely to different stimuli. Given this fact, it's outrageous to claim one particular system works equally well for everyone. You may find that my P.R.I.M.E.R. method works surprisingly well for you. Or you may find that a different approach, such as BSQ, OGSM, or the S.M.A.R.T.E.R. system, is more effective.

So let me make a proposal. Test drive my P.R.I.M.E.R. method for yourself. Put it through its paces. Follow my method, step by step, and note whether it produces positive results for you.

If you've read my other books or you're on my "productivity tips" email list, you know I strongly advocate personal experimentation. Don't assume your experiences will be the same as mine. Instead, test everything and evaluate the results according to how they impact your life and lifestyle.

I'm confident that my P.R.I.M.E.R. goal setting method will prompt you to take purposeful action that can literally transform your life. It can help you to discover new potential in yourself, inspire you to make bold commitments, and rack up impressive accomplishments.

It starts with a simple experiment. Try out my P.R.I.M.E.R. method. Give it a trial run, using a single goal as a test case. Follow the steps and monitor your progress. I have a feeling you'll be absolutely delighted with the results!

MAY I ASK YOU A SMALL FAVOR?

∾

First and foremost, thank you for taking the time to read *The P.R.I.M.E.R. Goal Setting Method*. I hope it was an enjoyable experience that offered actionable insights that'll have a positive impact on your life.

If anything in this book resonated with you, I'd love it if you would leave a review for it on Amazon. Reviews may not matter to big-name authors like David Allen, Timothy Ferriss, and Ray Dalio, but they're a *tremendous* help for little guys like myself. They help me to grow my readership by encouraging folks to take a chance on my books.

Second, if you'd like to be notified when I release new books (typically at a steep discount), please sign up for my mailing list at:

http://artofproductivity.com/free-gift/

You'll receive immediate access to my 40-page PDF guide *Catapult Your Productivity: The Top 10 Habits You Must Develop To Get More Things Done*. You'll also receive action-able advice on beating procrastination, creating morning routines, avoiding burnout, developing razor-sharp focus, and more!

If you have questions or would like to share a produc-tivity tip that has made a measurable difference in your life, please feel free to reach out to me at damon@artofproduc-tivity.com. I'd love to hear from you!

Until next time,

Damon Zahariades
http://artofproductivity.com

OTHER BOOKS BY DAMON ZAHARIADES

The Art of Letting GO

Finally let go of your anger, regrets, and negative thoughts and enjoy the emotional freedom you deserve!

The Mental Toughness Handbook

The definitive, step-by-step guide to developing mental toughness! Exercises included!

To-Do List Formula

Finally! Discover how to create to-do lists that work!

The Art Of Saying NO

Are you fed up with people taking you for granted? Learn how to set boundaries, stand your ground, and inspire others' respect in the process!

The Procrastination Cure

Discover how to take quick action, make fast decisions, and finally overcome your inner procrastinator!

Fast Focus

Here's a proven system that'll help you to ignore distractions, develop laser-sharp focus, and skyrocket your productivity!

The 30-Day Productivity Plan

Need a daily action plan to boost your productivity? This 30-day guide is the solution to your time management woes!

The 30-Day Productivity Plan - VOLUME II

30 MORE bad habits that are sabotaging your time management - and how to overcome them one day at a time!

How to Make Better Decisions

Learn how to finally overcome indecision and make smart, effective choices without fear or regret!

The Time Chunking Method

It's one of the most popular time management strategies used today. Triple your productivity with this easy 10-step system.

80/20 Your Life!

Achieve more, create more, and enjoy more success. How to get more done with less effort and change your life in the process!

Small Habits Revolution

Change your habits to transform your life. Use this simple, effective strategy for adopting any new habit you desire!

Morning Makeover

Imagine waking up excited, energized, and full of self-confidence. Here's how to create morning routines that lead to explosive success!

The Joy Of Imperfection

Finally beat perfectionism, silence your inner critic, and overcome your fear of failure!

Digital Detox

Disconnect to reconnect. Discover how to unplug and enjoy a more mindful, meaningful, and rewarding life!

For a complete list, please visit

http://artofproductivity.com/my-books/

ABOUT THE AUTHOR

Damon Zahariades is a corporate refugee who endured years of unnecessary meetings, drive-by chats with coworkers, and a distraction-laden work environment before striking out on his own. Today, in addition to being the author of a growing catalog of time management and productivity books, he's the showrunner for the productivity blog ArtofProductivity.com.

In his spare time, he shows off his copywriting chops by powering the content marketing campaigns used by today's growing businesses to attract customers.

Damon lives in Southern California with his beautiful, supportive wife and their frisky dog. He's currently staring down the barrel of his 50th birthday.

www.artofproductivity.com

Printed in Great Britain
by Amazon

12240041R00098